"Mark Miller's *Making Moral Choices, An Introduction* is a wonderful book for introducing young people to the many dimensions of decision making. Unlike some texts, it does not provide a series of analyses and answers. Rather it invites the young person to assume this responsibility and grow in the art of moral living. Miller's work is a fine educational instrument."

Richard A. McCormick, S.J.
John A. O'Brien Professor of Christian Ethics
University of Notre Dame

"In a time of moral confusion, Mark Miller resists the temptation to add one more voice to the babel of conflicting ethical systems. Instead, he offers young (and not so young) readers the wherewithal to build a personal foundation of analysis, insight, and criticism. Though he addresses specific issues and concrete cases, he is more interested in showing what goes into wise decision making and helping students develop the skills needed to find their way through the moral maze.

"This is an unusual book: one rooted in conviction, respectful of diversity, and committed to helping young people achieve the kind of enlightenment that issues in responsible living."

James DiGiacomo, S.J.

"That secret little voice inside isn't the key to making good decisions; instead, try knowledge, reflection, reason, dialogue, and faith! That's the essential message of *Making Moral Choices*.

"Wisely, the author doesn't rush to give 'right answers' to today's technological life-death dilemmas. Instead, he describes a process, offering ethical and moral principles and probing the impact of family, community, peers, and society on how we make decisions. Excellent reflection questions and group exercises help to make this a valuable resource, aimed at young people but important also for adults."

Valerie Vance Dillon
Family Life Minister
Author, *Becoming a Woman*

"In this refreshing book, the author uses the method—familiar from the Gospels—of conveying profound insights through the use of vivid analogies and contemporary examples.

"By respecting the integrity of his readers and conferring on them the dignity of responsibility, the author will appeal to a wide range of people who might not look at a conventional textbook on moral theology."

Joyce Poole, M.D.
Author, *The Harm We Do: A Catholic Doctor Confronts Church Moral and Medical Teaching*

"Mark Miller has produced a very welcome textbook in ethics for a course or program for young people. He sets out a course in applied ethics, less focused on particular moral decisions than on how moral decisions are reached. The course includes discussion of moral decision making based on principles, but it also includes discussion of the virtue and character ethics that has been receiving increased attention from Christian ethicists.

"The appeal of this very useful book is the absence of the jargon that infects too many textbooks. The substance of recent writing by Catholic moralists is here; only the technical terminology is gone. Teachers and students will also appreciate Miller's apparent insight into and sympathy for the problems of young people. The study of ethics and the process of ethical decision making require thought and attention. This welcome text will help insightful teachers to stimulate both."

John P. Boyle
Professor, School of Religion
University of Iowa

► An Introduction

MAKING MORAL CHOICES

MARK MILLER, C.Ss.R.

TWENTY-THIRD PUBLICATIONS
Mystic, CT 06355

Twenty-Third Publications
185 Willow Street
P.O. Box 180
Mystic, CT 06355
(203) 536-2611
800-321-0411

ISBN 0-89622-666-2
Library of Congress Catalog Card Number 95-61146
Printed in the U.S.A.

CONTENTS

INTRODUCTION   1

CHAPTER ONE
THE MORAL LAW   5

CHAPTER TWO
PRINCIPLES, LAWS, COMMANDS   15

CHAPTER THREE
THE ROLE OF CONSCIENCE   28

CHAPTER FOUR
PATTERNS OF MORAL REASONING   40

CHAPTER FIVE
WE ARE SOCIAL CREATURES   58

CHAPTER SIX
THE FAITH DIMENSION   73

CONCLUSION   86

MAKING MORAL CHOICES

INTRODUCTION

The art of ethics is the art of living. I do not mean by this that the ethicist, that is, the person who knows a great deal about ethical theory, also knows the art of living. Rather, those people are truly living who are making good moral decisions in the day-to-day activities that comprise most of their lives, but also in those critical moments when great or urgent decisions are needed.

Does that sound odd? In our society do we not associate the phrase "really living" with those people who have loads of money and lots of "fun" opportunities on which to spend their cash? Indeed, we live in a world that is constantly asking us to consider what it means to "really live," and the advertising industry is relentless and pretty clear about the answers. But what does it mean to really live? Amidst so many possibilities today, which choices really bring life and meaning, and how are we to know?

Perhaps we need a bit of perspective on this matter. Imagine yourself in fifty years. Would you rather look back on your life's highpoint as the moment you stepped behind the wheel of your own bright red Ferrari, or the legacy of three or four of your own children now happily raising their own families? Obviously, these choices do not have to be mutually exclusive. At the moment, however, you are young. The world, your world of the next fifty or sixty years, lies before you. How do you make the choices that will give your life substance, fulfillment, meaning? I believe that good, or moral, choices have their own reward, providing us with the groundwork for an ultimate satisfaction in who we are and what we have done with our lives.

What You Already Do

The purpose of this book, then, is not to tell you some nice, neat moral decisions you should make. Rather, this guide hopes to assist you to reflect on what you already do when you try to make good choices. There will be some ethical theory because good theories give us a framework for thinking about our actions. Theory, especially in ethics, must be complemented by personal experience. However, personal experience must be more than what you alone have experienced. The personal experience of family, of friends, of heroes, of failures and, most particularly, of wise people comprises the material for teaching each new generation. Ethical theory that begins and ends in books can often bypass the messy reality of human life and seek to impose an intellectual order that substitutes tidy ethical choices for good ones.

Thus, ethics (doing and thinking about it) requires that you be attentive to who you already are, to the decisions that already mold your life, to the sources of those decisions and, then, to the possibilities that lie ahead as you continue to create yourself and influence your world by your decisions and actions.

Even more so, ethics demands that you pay attention to ethical people. Nobody, of course, is perfect. But good people are models for us when they make good decisions and when we can see how they make them. St. Francis of Assisi, for example, can (and often does) teach our whole world about respecting the environment. His own life, attitudes, and deeds have often been looked upon as quaint and saintly; but when one gets to know him, the reality of his decisions in the face of a tough, exploitative world of commerce are eye-openers for our even more competitive world today.

Throughout this guide, I propose to use a number of different situations as ethical examples. However, the majority of my examples will come from three areas, the first two delving into the experience of young adults and the third demanding an extra level of ethical reflection. Thus, I will use some ordinary, day-to-day situations to remind us of the ordinariness of moral choosing. I will also speak to the complications of parent-teenage relationships, for there is an added moral dimension in the task of the child to become an adult while the parent learns to trust the child with growing responsibility in making decisions. And, finally, I will draw from the field of medical ethics or, as it is sometimes called, bioethics. I will do this for three reasons.

Three Important Considerations

First, most young people have not had extensive experience within hospitals or nursing homes (except for volunteers and those with family experience of serious illness); consequently, the ethical issues may have a freshness to them that will allow more open-minded thought. And where individuals have had some experience, I hope it will be enlightening when they add their experiences to the discussions.

Second, ethics as an academic discipline has undergone an enormous expansion in recent years. There are traditional areas of ethical reflection: marriage and family life (including human sexuality), issues in social justice, Christian or biblical ethics, and philosophical ethics. Today, however, it seems as if every area of human endeavor has its own accompanying ethics, often with many subdivisions: business ethics, ecological ethics, health care ethics, liberation ethics (with specializations for the poor, for minorities, for women, for the handicapped), and social ethics. Obviously, if ethics has to do with good or bad choices and actions, then it should not be surprising that every area of human endeavor has an ethical dimension. What is perhaps surprising is that society has taken so long to focus its ethical reflection on many of these areas. Be that as it may, ethical reflection on medical issues has proven to be one of the richest fields of thought and dialogue today. Modern medicine forces us to ask many troubling questions about why we are doing what we are doing.

Third, medical ethics struggles with three of the most pressing aspects of being human. When does life begin? What is a healthy life? And what is the meaning of both dying and death? Traditional philosophical wisdom has grappled with these issues under a variety of forms; the drama of modern health care which can "start" babies in test tubes and keep brain-dead patients "alive" poses these questions in startlingly new ways.

So, read on. Do not look in this guide for answers to abstract questions. Look rather for all that touches your life and, in touching your life, forces you to think about what it is to be human and what it is to do, and be, good. Remember only that anyone can make decisions, but it takes courage, wisdom, humility, and commitment to make good ones. And it takes time. Moral development is a life-long project; it takes a lifetime to learn and practice what we are learning. Making moral choices in your life is not a pass-or-fail exam; it is the hard joy of really living through every nook and cranny of the years that you are given in your one great gift, your own life.

CHAPTER ONE

THE MORAL LAW

Ethics and Morality

The word "ethics" is often used to describe the theory or reflection concerning human choice and behavior. "Morality," on the other hand, tends to be associated with human actions we think of as good or bad. For example, a philosopher is said to study ethics; but a business person runs a good, or moral, business. In this guide, however, ethics and morality will be used to mean the same thing. While our actions and our decisions are ethical behavior, with this activity is a parallel and constant process of reflecting on what we do and why. Nor is this process restricted to philosophers. Parents are always trying to explain to their children what is right or wrong and, sometimes, why it is one or the other. Even youngsters playing ball are debating rules for their game and, sometimes, reasoning their way to new adaptations. Questions that ask what we should do or what we ought to do connect our thinking and our actions.

A Particular Case

Consider for a moment the dilemma that the parents of three teenagers find themselves in. The middle boy, who is 14, comes home from school downcast and in what looks like a very bad mood. He is uncommunicative, not even responding to his mother's greeting as he walks in the door. In an unusual move he heads straight for his room where he throws his books on his desk and then slams the door.

His mother draws the obvious conclusion that something is wrong. She knocks gently on his door and calls his name. From inside the room she hears her son's voice, possibly trying to hide the fact that he is crying; he tells her, "Leave me alone. There's nothing wrong!"

Knowing her son as well as she does, the mother respects his need for privacy and for time to work out some of what he is dealing with. She is nonetheless very worried and makes a mental note to tell her husband as soon as he arrives home from work. Perhaps together they can talk to their son and find out what the problem is.

When the father arrives home it is time for supper and everybody gathers around the table, including the middle boy. But he is quiet and withdrawn and he keeps his face lowered, looking only at his plate. A quiet supper takes place with an artificial conversation. After eating only half his supper, the troubled boy asks to be excused and returns to his room, closing the door behind him.

When supper is finished the parents go to the boy's room, knock on his door and, despite being told to go away, enter the room and ask what the problem is. It takes a bit of prodding, but the boy eventually tells them of being pushed around by a couple of bullies at school and being threatened with a beating if he does not produce a few dollars a week for "protection." The boy was not badly hurt, but he is very scared and does not know what to do. He did not want to tell his parents because he had been warned that if this came out, they would "get him sooner or later." Now, despite feeling some relief at having shared his burden with his parents, he is even more terrified because they both know and are obviously going to do something.

What should the parents do? What choices are available to them and what is the best response to this situation?

Most parents will think of one (or all) of three options. First, they might try to get the school authorities involved because their son has a right to a proper education without this kind of tyranny. Second, they might try to counsel the boy to handle it himself. This might involve ignoring the bullies, going himself to a favorite teacher and explaining the situation, or perhaps even gathering a few friends to meet the threat head on. This choice would depend upon the circumstances of the school, the bullies, the teachers, and the personality of the boy himself. Third, the parents might try to handle the situation themselves. Perhaps the father will confront the bullies himself. He might contact the parents of the bullies. Or he might ask the police to accompany him and help straighten things out.

Notice, however, what the son thinks of each of these solutions. The first will entail the public limelight but with no guarantee that it will not make the situation worse. The principal of the school might make a major issue of this or might simply shrug his shoulders out of helplessness and ask for "proof." The second possibility of the boy handling it himself probably sounds downright scary to him; he does not feel that he could ever meet the bullies on their own terms. And the third possibility would either embarrass him in front of his peers or expand the confrontation into a battle of families.

When the boy makes his fears known, other possibilities might begin to surface. Change schools; work quietly through community structures; invite the bullies and their families over for a barbecue and a chat. These suggestions may sound rather odd because most of us assume we have to confront a problem head on and find a solution, usually involving a sense of justice to counter mistreatment, as quickly as possible. Nonetheless, when the entire situation is taken into account—perhaps it is an inner-city school where some after-school programs are needed to absorb the extra energy of the students, and to teach them how to respect one another on a deeper level than the students seem able to learn in school—the possible choices expand surprisingly. What looks like one choice in the face of a relatively straightforward situation begins to become more complicated as the various persons involved are taken into account. Not only does the question "What is good for the son?" need to be answered; but is there not something that can be done for the bullies or even for the whole situation involving the school?

So what do the parents do? An easy answer does not present itself. From the perspective of ethics, to give an answer to this situation is first to face a host of other questions such as: What is the school situation? Can the school staff deal with this situation constructively and for the good of everyone involved? Does the local community need to be involved? How serious is the threat of the bullies and how quickly must the parents act? And, in the midst of these questions, the parents must be prepared to help their son deal with the fear and the reality of his humiliation in the best possible way.

When you look at this situation it is relatively easy to set up a framework for finding a proper answer to the family's situation. We might first gather the facts about the school, the neighborhood, the bullies, other student relationships, and the staff. Then we could sort out what looks like the best path and offer that as an appropriate solution.

Still, to say "They ought to do this" makes dozens of assumptions about what is the right or wrong thing to do in this situation. Looking at their situation from the outside, some of us might suggest meeting force with force, either by the parents or by the boy and his friends; others might suggest leaving it to the proper authorities (they should look into it; that is what they get paid for); and still others might attempt to change the structures of the school or the community so that such things would be less likely to happen again.

But is there a "right" answer for the parents? Or can we, for the most part, do no more than give them our advice and then trust them to make the best decision they can under the circumstances? After all, they know their son, his school, the neighborhood, and perhaps the staff. Of course, they will have their own prejudices, their own way of doing things (just like everyone who offers them advice). A father who believes in "standing up for yourself" might not be able to see other choices. A mother who is overprotective may demand a change of schools.

What would the ethicist or ethical reflection add to the family? Not a final decision. Only the parents, and their son, in their understanding of all the factors of this situation can make the final choice. What an ethical reflection can possibly do is help them avoid bad decisions (responding with guns or another form of violence), perhaps explore more creative and positive resolutions, and make sure that the situation has been understood as fully as possible. For example, questioning the bullies may show that they were copying something on television and they only need a good lecture to get over such foolishness.

This family's quandary is one tiny slice out of the daily drama of human life. The parents *will* make their decision to the best of their ability. And they will be able to reflect on it with a little more balance after the consequences are known.

Let us hope, however, that our brief reflection on what is involved in their decision will give some idea of how interconnected we humans are and how complex are the choices we are called to make. Decisions are not made out of a vacuum. Nor do human actions just happen. We all come to our world with a certain way of understanding, of seeing things, of judging good from bad, and of investing ourselves. When humanity began on this planet, there was no instruction manual supplied to tell us exactly where everything goes and how it all fits together.

What was given to us was a very profound and subtle ability to think. Learning how to speak as infants has been accompanied for us by an ever-increasing ability to think our way through the thousand tasks of daily life that every human being encounters. Thinking itself has been mapped out in a zillion different books covering a million different areas of human endeavor. But, again, no blueprint exists for our thinking by which we can make designer decisions. We must learn to be the person we would praise as good or moral by the daily exercises of making good choices.

Making "Good" Choices; Making "Moral" Choices

An experienced fly fisherman may start the day with his favorite lure. But if there is no response, he pays close attention to what the fish might be attracted to. He may even have to take time off from fishing to fashion a special lure that simulates their current food. The fisherman is trying to "think like a fish"—which is a rather odd expression because no one has any idea how a fish thinks. Still, we do know how fish are liable to behave and so the good fisherman adjusts his plan of action accordingly.

Now, whether a fish rises to take a well-fashioned lure or not, we are not tempted to speak of the fish's action as good or bad. The fish just does what it does. On the other hand, we may have some very strong notions about the fisherman's actions. We may admire his skill, for example, unless we find out that he is fishing out of season or in a spot protected for spawning. In that case and despite his skill, we would call his action bad. A true fisher would be even more horrified if this person put his rod aside and used a stick of dynamite to ensure that he caught a fish. Whatever a sport fisher is, this fellow would not qualify.

Nonetheless, here we have the first clues to ethical theory. The fish does not make free choices. The human being does. Furthermore, every human being seeks to accomplish some good by his or her choices. Even the dishonest fisherman thinks he is doing something good for himself, namely, getting the fish regardless of the method used. Why would the rest of us, then, say that what he was doing was wrong? After all, with a little patience and care, he could probably catch his limit. And what difference does it make at the end of the day if he cheated a little to get to the same result?

The Purpose: Choices Aim for Something

Thus the first important distinction for ethics involves clarifying the purpose, or goal, of an action as opposed to the means used to attain this goal. We do not think of a fisherman as having any right to bring home a number of fish at the end of the day just because he has gone fishing. Fishing itself is a goal with its own internal rules or expectations (and some societal restrictions through laws). These rules protect the fish stocks, give the fish a chance (so to speak), and make fishing a skill rather than something like a commercial venture where the results can be counted and literally evaluated in dollars and cents. Unfair means for catching fish are then immoral because they jeopardize fish stocks and often the environment, and because they change the meaning of sport fishing. A good fisher does not come home with fish. A good fisher uses skills to catch the often elusive fish in a contest that allows the fish a possibility to survive through the use of its natural skills.

Two questions likely arise at this point. First, who made all the rules about sport fishing? And, second, what if the fisher needed the fish for food, as among the Eskimos? To the first question, I think it would be reasonable to answer that the notion of sport fishing has developed over many years according to the input of true sport fishers, conservation personnel, business interests, and environmentalists, including scientists. The ethics of sport fishing has similarly developed as the purpose of sport fishing has evolved and as the limited number of fish has become clearer. Matching wits, so to speak, with a rainbow trout rather than ensuring the catch of the fish by any means gives a clear goal by which the rules and ethics of sport fishing are composed.

As to the second question, Eskimos have their own methods of fishing that meet the food needs of their people. Their purpose, or goal, is not sport, despite any pleasure they may experience in catching the fish. The notion of "fishing" has two different meanings in these two contexts. Interestingly, the prowess of being a good fisher or hunter is extremely important in Eskimo society—but the prestige is based upon the skillfulness (which will produce results) rather than the results themselves.

A Final Reflection: Ends and Means

Life, for all its beauty, can at times be frustratingly complicated. Thus, we need to take a moment to ask ourselves about the goals, or ends, of our decisions, particularly in light of the principle that "the end does not justify the means." At the simplest level, if I am hungry and wish to quell my hunger, I may raid the refrigerator and eat whatever I choose. The goal is simple, to overcome my hunger. The means, one of several options, are also simple: Go to the "fridge" and pick something that is available and satisfying.

However, what if my goal is to ensure that my family always has enough food for its daily needs? That is, in order for you to raid the refrigerator, somebody has to implement a number of choices about a job, buying groceries and a refrigerator, setting up a dwelling, and so on, in order to make your simple choice even possible. The means one uses for such complicated choices often connect with life choices that are anything but simple: getting married and having children, settling in a job and a location, following a lifestyle. A number of different ends, or goals, may then be operative at the same time: providing for one's family, loving one's spouse, having a satisfying job. But not all the means will necessarily work toward fulfilling all the goals. I may have to stay, for example, in an unsatisfactory job in order to provide for my family. Is it immoral, then, to stay in an unsatisfactory job if my goal is to have a satisfactory one? Under the circumstances, one can hope for something better, but we would not speak of an immoral choice here (presumably because an unsatisfactory job is not evil, unlike stealing rather than working for the sake of my family). One goal predominates: care for one's family. Goals are themselves evaluated in relation to one another.

However, this raises a tough question. Are there any goals in life that override or direct all our actions? In the tradition of Aristotle, *the* goal of human life was conceived to be "happiness" (a rather flexible notion, one must admit). St. Thomas Aquinas and the Christian tradition took this idea one step further by suggesting that true happiness lay only in doing the will of God. This, then, could become the one overarching goal, or purpose, of a human life. If we could only see all our choices in the light of God's plan for us, then we could order all our means to this single, good purpose.

Life, of course, is not so simple. Nor is it always easy to figure out what God's will is, especially in every particular situation of our lives. Nevertheless, if we view our lives and our choices in this light—striving to do and to be what God wants of us—then we always have a reference point for evaluating our choices. Some will obviously be wrong, or bad, because they cannot possibly conform to what God would ask of us (stealing from children, or torture, or murder). The rest of our choices will, then, have to find a path of wisdom to understand what God asks and how we are to respond. And that brings us back to ethical reflection.

So, perhaps a saying of Mohandas Gandhi, the Indian prophet of nonviolence, will now make some sense. "Means," he says, "are ends in the making." If the final end is union with God, every choice along the way contributes to the "making."

Questions for Reflection and Discussion

1. What is the purpose, or goal, of the parents' deliberation about their son's quandary? Why do they need to think about possible courses of action?

2. Can their deliberation be reduced to one purpose, or are there several at work? What are they and how are they related to each other (that is, e-value-ated, or valued by the parents)?

3. What are the means available to the parents to attain their final purpose? Are they all (equally) ethical? Which means is "better" than the others? How do you know this?

4. There is a famous principle in ethics, "The end does not justify the means." Does this make sense to you? Can you think about this principle without using examples? What does this tell you about the role of experience in learning to make moral decisions? Pick several examples from you own life and see if you can understand how the principle is applied in daily life.

5. Can you give an example from your life where the end was clearly what you wanted but the means seemed unethical? What did you (would you) do?

An Exercise

Break into groups of five or six. Have one student in each group think of an incident in his or her life where a relatively tough decision had to be made. Have that student present the situation without saying what was finally decided. Let the other group members discuss the situation and attempt to list the answers to these questions:

1. Do we understand the whole situation? Are there any questions that need to be asked in order to make sure that the entire situation is clear? Have we got the facts straight?

2. What possible courses of action or response can we think of? (Do not judge whether these possibilities are good or bad; just record them.)

3. What are the pros and cons of each choice? What are the consequences, good and bad, as far as you can determine?

4. Are there any choices that look attractive but include something that makes you uneasy (violence, dishonesty, etc.)? Compare the attractive aspects with the bad side.

As a group, decide on the best possible choice and defend that to the one who presented the story.

Let the presenter then tell what, in fact, he did and why. Compare this with what the group suggested. Are there any differences? What accounts for them?

For Further Reading

Böckle, Franz. *Fundamental Moral Theology.* New York: Pueblo, 1980. (A thorough and profound examination of the most basic elements of moral theology.)

Hallett, Garth L. *Christian Moral Reasoning: An Analytic Guide.* Notre Dame, IN: University of Notre Dame Press, 1983. (One moral thinker's in-depth analysis of the various aspects of moral choices and actions.)

Hamel, Ronald P., and Kenneth R. Himes, eds. *An Introduction to Christian Ethics: A Reader.* New York and Mahwah, NJ: Paulist Press, 1989. (A superb collection of articles on many aspects of moral reasoning from a Christian perspective.)

O'Connell, Timothy E. *Principles for a Catholic Morality.* Rev. ed. San Francisco: Harper & Row, 1990. (A thorough examination of a systematic moral theology.)

CHAPTER TWO

PRINCIPLES, LAWS, COMMANDS

In the previous chapter I referred to the sentence "The end does not justify the means" as a principle. A commonly heard phrase is "acting on principle," as when a politician proclaims that he or she will vote "according to the principle of the matter," or one person sues another "for the sake of the principle, not the money." Principles seem to be mighty important guidelines for us. How, then, do they fit into our moral education?

The Language of Morality

To ask about principles is to ask a deeper question concerning our very ways of speaking about morality. In short, if you were asked to present an ethical guide for some field of human endeavor, what "language" would you use? Think of any sport, say, a basketball or hockey game. How would you outline for a newcomer what is "right" or "wrong" in playing the game? Traditionally, the language of ethics has been the language of law. Accordingly, you would tell the newcomer the rules of the game.

Ethical thought, ethical guidelines, ethical commands, and the like can generally be summarized in law formulas. Laws will tell us what is right or wrong, thereby giving us a relatively clear picture of how to judge our actions. For example, if the law dictates that the premeditated ending of another's life, except in war, is murder, then everybody in society understands that to kill another human being is both wrong and liable for punishment. Note that the same is true for the "language" of behavior in basketball; if you hold the opposing player in the midst of the game, you are breaking the rules and are liable to be penalized. The language of law or rules provides us with directives, or guidelines, for our choices and actions.

There are, obviously, different kinds of laws. The rules of basketball are quite different from the rules of criminal law. Further, some people who break one or other of society's laws will claim that they are following a "higher law," perhaps the moral law or the law of God. While there may be arguments about which laws are most basic, we may note that the language used is still that of law.

The Rule of Law for a Country

The language of law is one attempt to articulate guidelines for human behavior. Society tends to formulate laws according to what is best for all its citizens amidst the tangled web of our interconnected lives. Societal laws are a balance of criminal law (to prevent or punish wrongdoing) and civil laws (to regulate interactions and exchanges concerning property, business, taxes, etc., among people). However, all of us know that some of any society's laws are good, many are controversial, and some are simply bad. Does the fact that they are laws mean they have to be obeyed anyway?

One of the great struggles of modern nations has been an attempt to articulate a framework within which ordinary laws make sense. Accordingly, most governments or nations create a Constitution and, perhaps, a Bill, or Charter, of Rights. Such documents specify the guarantees that a "constitutional government" must abide by in the treatment of all its citizens. Not only do such documents prevent abuse by arbitrary and willful governments, but they also force lawmakers to think of the implications of their proposed laws in the broadest context of what is right for each member of society. Thus, a local law prohibiting a certain ethnic group from living in one part of a city would be ruled unconstitutional where the Constitution demands that all citizens be treated as equals.

Principles of the Moral Law

The laws of a country give us one important perspective on the moral law. If we consider the moral law as the full spectrum of guidelines for good human behavior, then we shall recognize that there are many different kinds of law lumped together under the notion of the moral law.

To begin, we can return to our word "principles" and recognize that principles play an analogous role to a Constitution or Charter of Rights. Principles provide us with broad statements concerning what it means to be a good human being. They are often expressed as commands or exhortations, in part because their authors acknowledge our freedom to follow, or obey, them. "Be honest!" is a good example of a principle for guiding one's life. "Be true to yourself," "Be loving," "Follow God's commands," and the like tell us in very general ways how to live and make our decisions. These are, then, principles for a good, or moral, life, exhorting a daily behavior that strives to embody these high-minded ideals.

Prohibitions of the Moral Law

Interestingly, principles can be "turned around" such that they take on the context of prohibitive laws. For many of us, this is the most common experience of law. "Do not lie," "Do not hate your fellow human being," "You shall not steal," or "Do not worship false gods"—all echo in our minds as describing actions to avoid. These negative commands, though, may mean many different things to different people. For example, they may seem to be less principles for living than commands about "forbidden zones." At times, until we understand what it is that is bad for us (and why), these forbidden zones are often enticing precisely because they are forbidden!

Ironically, some laws may have this odd effect of making what is evil look attractive. That often happens when law is seen or felt as simply something imposed on us by an arbitrary lawgiver. The imposed law may not resonate with our sense of self or with our knowledge (however limited) of what is good for us and what is not. We can, of course, obey the law because it is the law; but we may also find ourselves looking for loopholes or even rejecting the whole law because we really want something else.

Moral Law for All Human Beings

And that brings us back to the most basic question about the moral law. Where does it come from? Or, more simply, how do we know that various laws are, in fact, good? And, ultimately, why should we obey the moral law?

In traditional Catholic thought the moral law was always understood to have come from God. Because God is all good, the law from God for human beings had to be good as well. However, centuries of experience led thinkers to understand that God's *revealed* law, which we recognize through the Scriptures, is a complex mixture of moral laws (holding for all human beings), ritual laws (for the Temple priests of the Old Testament), purity laws (for the people of Israel), and human interpretations about how to live. By the thirteenth century, the time of Thomas Aquinas, for example, many of these latter classes of laws were no longer adhered to within the Christian community. On the other hand, new laws at all levels had developed or been discovered in the Christian tradition. Even without direct Scriptural reference, many of these laws made great sense. But the question was then raised, how do we know that they are from God, that they reflect God's will for us?

Natural Law

Reflecting upon God's law for human beings and upon the ability of "pagans" to state more or less accurately many of the laws for human behavior in ways that echoed God's laws, thinkers like Aquinas spoke of the *natural law* that God had fashioned into the very fabric of created reality. Today we tend to think of the natural law in terms of the physical laws of the universe, laws that are proven in physics, chemistry, astronomy, biology, and the like. What

Aquinas meant, however, was that God had so fashioned the world that the laws guiding all the activities of all created beings are somehow built into the nature of these beings.

This is easy to see, for example, in the law of gravity; but it is less obvious in the laws of human living. Still if an apple "must" fall out of a tree when the conditions are right, then it is not hard to see how human beings "must" try to be honest in their dealings with one another. Of course, we have given two different meanings to the word "must" here, so perhaps it is not so easy to see the connection. The law of gravity operates regardless of what humans think. However, the moral law of honesty always remains an ideal or an exhortation or a principle because human beings have the freedom to follow the law or not. What is important about the natural law is that it claims that a human being is only truly or fully human—or good—when he or she follows the moral law, which is the law appropriate for human behavior.

Human Nature: Freedom for the Good

Human beings recognize within their very nature a gift, or an aspect, called freedom. If I am in the apple tree, I have a choice whether to climb down or jump. Many factors may influence my decision, such as whether I am a daredevil; but freedom is inherent in my final decision and subsequent action. Accordingly, notes Aquinas, the natural law sees freedom as part of the nature of being human. He then goes on to ask what it is that guides our freedom to make the right choices. The basic answer is "the good." We are actually created to choose the good. It is our nature. It is the natural goal of our freedom. Hence, the most fundamental or general command of the natural law is "Do good, avoid evil." This is called the first principle of the natural law and holds for every possible situation in which a human being can make a choice.

Freedom: Knowledge and Will

If we were made to choose the good, why do we need any law to guide us? It is rather obvious, of course, that we do not always choose good over evil. Human beings struggle with two major issues: First, how do we know what is good? And, second, even when we know what is truly good, why do we not always choose it? The first question is a challenge for our intellect; understanding what is really good is not easy. A child standing in front of the candy counter thinks only of "good-for-me" ("I want this candy") rather than what is good for the child (honesty) or society (trust). Nonetheless, even a well taught youngster may stand before the candy counter and, knowing full well that stealing is wrong, may still take a piece of candy when the storekeeper isn't looking.

Carrying through on what we know, that is, ensuring that our doing is in sync with our knowing, is the second problem. Knowledge also requires an act of the will to become a deed. And as dieters or those trying to quit smoking will attest, will power is quite different than knowledge.

Where does the moral law fit into this picture? The moral law, to oversimplify, is humanity's attempt (and, for believers, God's gift) to help us both understand right from wrong and to encourage our wills to choose right over wrong. The moral law is not a taskmaster forcing us to follow its will. Rather, it is an expression of human (and divine) wisdom that guides us in our decisions. While we can discover much of the moral law within our own being and experience (I can find out the hard way, for example, what the consequences of lying will be), other humans have already made considerable discoveries and expressed them for the benefit of all. Think of what it means to follow the guidelines of wisdom (rather than just the dictates of law), that is, of the people who have learned from experience. Then, perhaps, you will better understand the significance of the moral law.

Moral Law as a System of Laws

Many people speak of the moral law as if it were a clear, unambiguous set of guidelines given to humanity to follow without too many questions. The image of Moses bringing the two tablets with the Ten Commandments down the mountain fits this notion perfectly.

However, as I am using the "moral law," I am attempting to capture all the levels of guidance we human beings use for good decisions and behavior. Such an interpretation would then include those laws that hold for all human beings all the time (for example, "It is always wrong to kill willfully another innocent human being") and those laws (or rules or norms) that are developed to help in the particular situations of human beings. For example, the rules of the classroom which are to promote an atmosphere of learning, or the business rules developed by a company to ensure honest business, or even the rules of etiquette at the dinner table—all fit under the notion of the moral law.

Of course, some rules then become more important, or more universal, or more morally appropriate than others. For myself, I am not going to spend much time debating the rules of etiquette; I am far more interested in what makes us human, or what makes our sexuality human, or what medical decisions are truly human. I might add, however, that reading a book on etiquette may provide some fascinating insights into how human beings "do what is right" in certain formal or informal situations and how "uncomfortable" or "wrong" people may feel when they break such rules!

Given this understanding, I would like to conclude by suggesting that the natural law in its broadest sense becomes, then, the "law of right reason." To oversimplify, this means that we must be able to find the right, or good, action to do in every situation, according to the best use of our reason. That, of course, raises an enormous question: "What is right reason?" And rather than answer that question or get into the many debates about the meaning of natural law, I refer the reader back to the ways you use your reason in your own daily life and experiences. Attentiveness on that level, it is hoped, will allow for the deeper philosophical questions about the natural law or the moral law to arise as part of the awareness itself.

Kinds of Law

When we talk about principles, laws, rules, and commands as the language of law, we must also remember the different kinds of laws that are included in such a broad and complex classification. When your mother tells you not to steal, you can be certain that this is an important value she is communicating to you. When she also tells you that you should wear a hat in winter, you instinctively know that this is a different kind of command dealing with an issue that is less serious than the first (unless, of course, you catch a cold and die of pneumonia. Mothers know!).

1. Principles

Principles are the most fundamental guidelines that are given to us (whether by God or in accord with nature or as discovered in traditional human wisdom). They provide the most basic directions for living our lives in ways that are called good. To be an honest person, and therefore trustworthy, is a way of life a person must choose each day, especially when particularly attractive opportunities for dishonesty present themselves. One may lie to gain an advantage, to protect oneself, or out of laziness or selfishness. The honest person learns how to avoid such traps and is then a living example of the principle. (We might note, too, how "living examples" teach us a great deal more about being honest than a bald, moral statement does.)

2. Laws and Rules

Laws and rules are generally more specific commands that hold in most instances. A traditional example is found in the rule "Always return borrowed property." That is an important rule to live by. But if you have borrowed your neighbor's shotgun and he now demands it back but with the obvious intent of hurting someone, it would be moral for you to refuse to return the borrowed gun. We might add that a higher principle is involved, namely, your responsibility for the safety of some innocent person. The higher principle does not invalidate the moral rule; rather, it provides a broader perspective that prevents a form of legalist interpretation of more specific rules.

3. Understanding the Levels of Law

Most of society's laws are a mixture of basic principles and rules that preserve order and harmony in society. Red traffic lights demand that approaching vehicles stop. There is an inherent sensibility to everybody obeying the rule. Otherwise, dangerous chaos would rule the roads. A rare exception might still occur, however, if a husband were driving his wife, already in labor, to the hospital. He must still be very cautious at red lights (the others on the roads do not know his predicament). But if nobody else is in the way or ready to go through the opposing green light, he need not wait for the light to change before proceeding. Rules provide us with the presumption of right action. Thus, breaking a rule or making an exception always puts the burden of proof on the one who presumes to go against the rule. A police officer will understand the husband's reason for driving through a red light. The same officer would suddenly turn deaf to a young woman's pleas that there was no point in waiting at the light (only) because there was no other traffic coming. Such behavior may not appear dangerous in this instance, but it increases the probability of taking one chance too many and causing a serious accident later.

4. Context for More Specific Laws

Laws and rules often have to be seen in their context before their wisdom is understood. Parents make rules for their children because children, including teenagers, do not always realize the consequences of their choices. (Parents, by the way, often do not speak about the rules that they impose on themselves. They simply live the wisdom they have chosen; for instance, not spending more than they earn, ensuring that the children are fed, clothed, and educated, remaining faithful to their jobs for the sake of the family, and so on.) Following the rules of parents is important.

So is questioning those rules if they seem unfair, or as you grow older and you presumably become more responsible. Nonetheless, the best advice for teens is to realize that taking the consequences of your own choices is often the hardest thing in the world to do. Making decisions is easy. Being there to pick up the pieces and claim responsibility makes you an adult (and not even all adults fit this description). Thus, should you choose to break a rule, even if you think you have a good reason, be prepared to be honest with yourself and your parents by taking the consequences. That way you will discover whether or not you are trying to be moral (that is, doing what you believe is right and good). After all, if the husband goes through the red light and causes an accident, he will be charged for breaking the law—for he did not do so safely. Remember, too, that if you stay out late at night and are grouchy or unreceptive at school the next day, others are paying the consequences for your decisions.

A Final Reflection: Wisdom Includes the Law

To conclude this chapter, it might be helpful to think of morality less in terms of laws (though these remain important) and more in terms of wisdom. Wisdom suggests that the intelligent and morally courageous person chooses what is right even if there is no law. There is a famous story of a Greek philosopher who was asked how he would live his life if the barbarians currently threatening Greece took over. He answered, "I shall not change a thing. I would continue to live what I know and now live as right." That is wisdom.

Questions for Reflection and Discussion

1. What are some of the main principles that function in our society? That is, what standards or expectations about "doing good and avoiding evil" do you see around you? (Are these principles easy to put into words? Can they be phrased in different ways? Does the phrasing make a difference?)

2. Do you personally share these principles? Name four principles that are important guidelines in your life. Is there any conflict with some of the principles of society you named?

3. What are the "rules" in your home? How do they relate to any of the principles you have already outlined?

4. What are some "religious principles" in your life or family? Where do they come from? How do they differ from society's principles?

5. Can you think of a law that is a bad or dumb law? Can you think of a law that does some good but also has some bad effects? Can you reformulate the law so that the bad effects are diminished? Does this change the intent of the law?

6. Write down one law of physics, one from biology, and a moral law. Why are they all called "laws"? What are the key differences between them?

7. Suppose you were a king and could only make one law for your people. What would it be? Why that law?

Exercise 1: Kinds of Law

Find a copy of the Ten Commandments. Then draw up a list of ten rules that are operative in your classroom or among your group. These latter rules may be explicit ("No smoking") or implicit and unspoken. For example, you may have never had heard anyone say "No throwing objects," but the rule effectively is in place in your classroom. Notice that I have phrased this rule, like most of the Ten Commandments, as a negative command. However, just as the fourth commandment is a positive demand ("Honor your mother and Father"), so try to make some of your rules similarly positive. (For example, "Look after the person who appears to be having a health problem.")

a. Compare the two lists of rules. What is the difference between them? List a half dozen differences if you can.

b. What values are the negative commands trying to protect? For example, "You shall not steal" protects private property and commands trust among people. (Notice how the positive values are often an explanation for the reasonableness of the command or rule. Notice, too, how many different positive values can be thought of when explaining the reasonableness of the law.)

c. Try turning the commands and rules around, making them all positive. How easy is it, then, to follow these commands compared with the negative ones? What is the difference?

d. Pick one commandment and one rule. Can you think of a possible exception to either one that you are able to justify? What does this tell you both about the relative importance of the two types of law and the process of justifying an exception?

e. What is the difference between knowing a law or commandment, and being convinced of its truth? Test this out on the ten rules you gathered.

Exercise 2: Who Makes the Rules and Why?

A fascinating, though imperfect, analogy may be drawn between the natural law given to all human beings to guide them through life and the system of laws, rules, or guidelines that parents give their children to guide them into adulthood. Parents, of course, are not God, so their moral-law-for-their-children will never be perfect. Still, reflection on your own upbringing can be very revealing about the place and meaning of the various kinds of laws in our lives.

a. What are some of the principles—the foundational commitments—your parents try to live by? How do they communicate these principles to you? That is, what language do they use? Is there sometimes a difference between their (stated) principles and their actual living of them? Why?

b. Parents will sometimes repeat as rules what they believe are simply moral laws (given to them by their tradition, or faith, or upbringing). For example, they might teach you that sex is to be saved for marriage. Forget for a moment whether or not you agree with the statement. This is not a test on obedience to the law. Rather, if this is an important principle, what *understanding* of human beings is it trying to communicate? How would this principle look as a negative command? As a positive command? What are the values it seeks to uphold? If you understand what this principle is trying to communicate, does that make it easier to follow? Why or why not?

c. Sometimes parents make what could be called "contextual laws," rules that have no internal necessity but the parents judge them suitable to the context of their children's lives. For example, parents may establish a midnight curfew on Friday nights. What are their reasons for such a rule? Are the reasons good ones? What alternatives might there be to such rules, alternatives that would accomplish the same purpose? What kind of rules are these in comparison to principles?

d. Teens often talk about their parents (not) trusting them. What difference would that make for the moral rules their parents offer? Would parents make fewer rules where there is greater trust? Why? Would the rules make more sense? Why? Would the very notion of rules change with greater trust? (Think, perhaps, of older brothers and sisters who are beyond high school. What changes in their relationship with their parents? What "rules" do they take with them?)

e. Now use your imagination, which is one of the best and least used helps for good choices. Think of some situation where your parents have gotten on your case, perhaps forbidden you to do something or go somewhere. In a small group pour out your side of the story, what you think of their rule and why. Now let the rest of the group imagine that they are your parents and have to provide the guidance. What would the group say to you from the parents' perspective? Be honest (there's one of those moral principles popping up unexpectedly in an ordinary situation). Don't twist the story to suit your present circumstances!

Is there a certain prejudice in your interpretation of any rule? Are you dealing, then, with what is right or what you want? What does this exercise tell you about being ethical?

For Further Reading

Dwyer, John C. *Foundations of Christian Ethics.* New York and Mahwah, NJ: Paulist Press, 1987. (This book has a good chapter on moral norms. It also sets reflection on moral norms in the broader context of other aspects of moral thinking. The final chapter on "Conscience" is also very instructive.)

Gula, Richard M. *What Are They Saying About Moral Norms?* New York and Ramsey, NJ: Paulist Press, 1982. (A good summary of the role of moral norms and the limits of thinking only with norms.)

McNamara, Vincent. *Love, Law & Christian Life: Basic Attitudes of Christian Morality.* Wilmington, DE: Michael Glazier, 1988. (The places of law, love, and the Scriptures for the moral life of Christians are looked at in depth.)

Wadell, Paul C. *The Primacy of Love: An Introduction to the Ethics of Thomas Aquinas.* Mahwah, NJ: Paulist Press, 1992. (A fascinating look at love as the primary "moral norm" for ethics; love is both a principle and a living reality. Though somewhat technical, the book gives an excellent rendition of Aquinas's insights into the moral life as far more than following the law.)

CHAPTER THREE

THE ROLE OF CONSCIENCE

When I was a youngster I do not ever recall being told, "Follow your conscience!" While my parents, teachers, and priests phrased their rules in different ways, I was simply told to obey them, to do as they said. The rules were pretty clear for us and one either followed them (and was "good") or did not follow them—in which case you got a reputation!

Your Conscience

Today, the role and place of conscience is much more prominent in discussions about morality. In situations of moral ambiguity a person may be admonished, "Follow your conscience." A clear blueprint of what is right or wrong is not available; you are then challenged to judge the situation as the circumstances change. For example, if your parents allow you to go to a party on the condition that drugs and alcohol will not be present and you tell them that a couple of kids may show up with booze but that won't affect the rest of the party-goers, your parents may invite you to follow your conscience about staying or leaving. Implicit in their permission is the trust that you will be able to see if the alcohol begins to affect the party adversely. They will then expect you to do the right thing and leave. If, however, the majority of the young people ignore the alcohol and the party carries on as planned, the appropriate decision will be to stay. In both cases, it is not a black-and-white law that is laid on you; you are called upon to make a mature judgment.

Appeals to conscience often evoke expectations. Parents may say to their children, "You have been brought up with a good set of values—to be honest, considerate, well mannered, and not to respond to evil with evil—please follow your conscience in applying these values." The parents are not clarifying their expectations by laying down more rules; they are telling you where to look when troublesome situations arise. Another way of saying this is, "We have taught you to be a certain kind of person; where you have to make your own choices (without our direct guidance or threat of punishment), we expect you to choose according to the kind of person we expect you to be."

Personal choice is an obvious component of conscience. Conscience implies that an individual has the capacity to make responsible, correct, and good choices on her or his own. A teenager is entrusted by a parent to make good decisions, but according to a well formed conscience. One may go so far as to say that any human being is entrusted by the Creator, who made us free, to make good choices, according to a well formed conscience.

What Is Conscience?

What, then, is a well formed conscience? Or, more simply, what is a conscience? Even asking the question this simply, however, may be misleading. For the question implies that we can look inside ourselves and find some thing we call a conscience. We may then be misled by some of the images or metaphors used to describe conscience. For example, some people will say that conscience is a voice inside us, or even the voice of God inside us, telling us what to do or not do. The implication is that we have only to wait for the voice to speak in order to know right from wrong. Other people will say that conscience is a feeling inside us; when a person feels strongly that something is right (or wrong), then that is our conscience giving us guidance. Still others, though this is less common today, will say that conscience is the obligation we feel that demands that we obey the law. Conscience in this view is right response to good law.

Now each of these images, or notions, gives us some insight into *how* conscience works, but they may also misdirect us if we assume that they tell us *what* conscience is. For conscience is not some thing either inside the person (neither a voice nor a feeling) nor outside you (the law) that tells you what to do. Very simply, conscience is really nothing other than *you striving to make the best choice you can* under the circumstances. It is the totality of your knowledge about what is right or good and your desire to do or be good. It operates in the actual choices you make each day, but is usually only felt when it raises troublesome questions about uncertain choices.

The pressure of conscience generally increases, the tougher the choices you face. You do not need much of a conscience to choose to be good to your friends; that is something you want to do. On the other hand, you may need a powerful boost from your conscience if you have an exam to study for and your friends want to play ball on a sunny afternoon. Conscience is that pull toward what is right even, or especially, when something attracts you in a different direction.

We may now see how the previously mentioned metaphors and ideas influence the meaning of conscience. Although not a voice, conscience acts like an inner voice, almost as if we are talking to ourselves—and this is especially true when our outer actions are not completely honest. Most times, when I tell a lie to someone, I *know* it is wrong and something inside me tells me so, even if I don't "hear" the words. Similarly, one could describe this unease as a feeling which, if I were to pay attention to it, would remind me that telling this lie is wrong. And, naturally, if I were to stop and think about the rule or principle "Be honest," I would clearly understand that I am doing something wrong. An inner voice or feeling, or a clear understanding of the moral law are all parts of a well-functioning conscience.

Informed Conscience

Often lost in the discussion of conscience is the education, or formation, each of us needs. One might recall the impoverished boys in Charles Dickens's story, *Oliver Twist.* They were taught to steal by the man who fed and looked after them. This authority figure was not teaching them about good and evil but training them to do what he wished. (The boys saw this as "good" from their perspective because he took care of them.) The disdain of other people, the threat of the police, and perhaps distant memories from families long gone might have made these boys feel that something was wrong. But until they understood that stealing was wrong (despite the perceived benefits), one could scarcely expect their consciences to convince them otherwise. Conscience does not operate in a vacuum (although some people who claim it is the voice of God might disagree). It grows and develops within the social context of a person's life. That is why it would be better phrasing to invite people to "follow your well formed conscience." Simply to "follow your conscience" may give the misleading impression that whatever your conscience justifies is necessarily good.

How, then, do we form our consciences? There are two major tasks to accomplish: knowledge and character formation.

Rules as Knowledge

If principles, laws, rules, and commands are the usual way for us to talk about morality, then we need to know what these are telling us about what is right and what is wrong. We need to understand how principles work, how laws (and different kinds of laws) work, how rules and commands are directed toward our choices and actions. For example, the Ten Commandments give an excellent sketch of fundamental principles for the moral life—but even they are quite varied in their expression and scope.

Although moral knowledge may be summarized in codes of laws and rules, morality itself is communicated and learned in a great variety of complex and interconnected ways. Parents and teachers may sometimes use rules and commands, often accompanied by explanations, encouragement, and threats; but rules and commands are not taught as if human beings were computers sharing data about how people operate.

Learning from People

The way that most of us learned right from wrong was through stories. Starting as very young children, we heard very simple stories, often with profound moral implications for our own lives. "The Ugly Duckling" and countless such Hans Christian Andersen tales taught us to look beyond the surface to discover what was most important. Think of how simple statements like "Be honest," "Be satisfied with who you are," and the like were and are part, or summaries, of these stories. Indeed, one could go a step further and say that watching our parents and other adults was also a way of learning from their stories, their example. When my father went next door to help our neighbor build his garage, notions of neighborliness and help were implanted in his children.

The Place of Stories

Gradually, as life grew more complicated, the stories that were part of our education also grew more complex, pointing out the ambiguities of life, focusing on life's gray areas and paradoxes. In stories one sees good and evil side by side; and, as in life, separating the two is often beyond our ability. Some stories show how evil does triumph over good. Others cleverly paint a picture of the flawed character or surprising depth of ordinary individuals. Within the messiness of life, the formation of conscience takes on all the hues of finding/choosing goodness in the midst of an often confounding and shadowy world.

Indeed, as one grows older, life itself forces its lessons upon us. The betrayal of a friend, the care of a teacher you thought did not like you, the realization that your parents are human, the failure of hopes and plans—life has a way of educating those who pay attention. And in the midst of all of our growing knowledge about life and its choices, perhaps we begin to see more clearly the wisdom contained in the guidance offered by the moral law (often embodied in our parents and teachers), as well as the difficulty we have in following this guidance, in being good.

Character Formation

And so, we need more than knowledge to have a well formed conscience. We need practice. This is what I mean by character formation. As important as it is to know what is right or wrong, we also have to have the courage or character to follow what we know. To know that gossip is wrong and often very harmful to people is one thing; to refuse to participate—which is an act demanding considerable character when you very much want your friends to like and accept you—means that "I practice what I preach." In short, knowledge only goes so far. Who I am says all the rest. If I am convinced, for example, of the two great commandments of Jesus, love God and love your neighbor as yourself (see Matthew 22:34–40), I display very little character and less conscience if I give God no time or attention, or if I pick on certain classmates because everybody else does.

Character formation means that I am willing to work on myself so that what I say and what I do are in harmony. It means that I have to struggle against tendencies to excuse myself ("Everybody does it"), to rationalize ("It wasn't so bad"), to go against what I know is right ("So what if it was wrong?"), or to give in to my laziness, cowardice, or selfishness.

Character Development

Each situation where I have to make a "character" choice either builds or takes away from my character, from who I am. When I was a newspaper delivery boy, I recall a customer paying me twice for one week's service. She trusted me to keep track of whether she had paid and I forgot. I will never forget the look on her face when I went back after checking my records and refunded her 35 cents (yes, that was a week's cost for the newspaper, a long time ago). As tempting as it was to keep the money ("Oh, she'll never miss it" and "Why make a fuss...?"), I learned more in that moment of her response about the trust that goes with honesty than I have learned from all the textbooks admonishing me to obey the law.

Daily Habits of Good Character

Character formation involves two related but distinct tasks. First, it means that we have to build good habits into our ways of making decisions. For example, if I learn to respond pleasantly to people, chances are that I will make more friends, find more opportunities in life, and avoid many painful responses. There is, of course, no guarantee that my pleasant response will bring the same in return. We might then remember something beyond pleasantness that Jesus taught: I do not respond in a friendly way only to get something good in return; no, I respond in that way in order to be the person I choose to be. Accordingly, if someone does not answer me in a friendly manner, that does not give me the right to change my approach because I feel hurt. I am responsible for *my* choices and for who *I* choose to be. Nobody can force me to be unfriendly; that is my choice. Nor can I blame someone else for changing my tune; that is still my choice.

As a further insight, we may note that sayings, especially the kind Jesus and other great figures coined, often capture a striking truth about how to live. "Turn the other cheek" may be a succinct way of saying what I just said. A saying is not a story, but it is another way of communicating what one *ought* to do or not do, that is, what is right or wrong.

Meeting New Challenges with Resources of Character

Second, if good habits are important and help us to respond almost instinctively in good ways, we must also remember that life is very good at throwing us curves. A powerful example can be seen in the lives of those husbands or wives who take care of a spouse with Alzheimer's disease. Gradually, the memory of the sufferer fades away to the point where he or she may not even recognize a long-loved spouse. The caregiver could then say "What's the point?" Invariably, however, as long as the sufferer is manageable, most spouses fall back on their own loving character, formed by many years of love and adaptation, and learn to love in ways that are profoundly different, often with no recognition at all from the one being helped.

A woman with Alzheimer's disease, for example, used to accuse her husband (and others) of stealing her things. Because she had lost her short-term memory, she could never remember where her things were. However, as her paranoia grew, she would actually hide things, thereby making it even more difficult for her husband to prove that the item was just mislaid. No amount of reasoning did any good (five seconds later she couldn't remember the reasons given). Meanwhile, the husband learned to suffer his wife's accusations without any response because a response would only agitate her more, while no answer at all would itself soon be forgotten. The husband's instinct to justify himself (an old habit!) gave way to his deeper understanding of his wife's condition and the need to adapt himself and his love to her.

Much of the learning in our schools and educational systems, unfortunately, concentrates on knowledge. Still, if we pay attention to people and the numerous situations we find ourselves in each day, we will often find that character formation can also be learned. The process, however, is much more subtle. Students learn from the patience of a particular teacher, or the concern of a coach, or the fidelity of a teacher who loves to teach. We all learn from our parents, from our friends, from people we admire. Despite all their weaknesses and foibles, people are still magnificent embodiments of so many of the good traits that are part of good character. It is from special people and ordinary people that we learn the meanings and the subtleties of such words as hope, courage, fidelity, forgiveness, staying power, honesty, passionate intensity, caring, sacrifice, and many more. Are these words a reality in your life? Are they found as a result of your moral choices? The goodness of people, when we stop to pay attention, is often overwhelming. And their example is certainly one of the gifts available to those who take their own character formation seriously.

A Final Reflection: The Place of Feelings

You may notice that this chapter begins to include a realm that is often uncomfortable for discussions: feelings. Most books on ethics tend to concentrate on the intellectual tasks of those who wish to understand ethics or principles or laws. Great discussions, even heated arguments, can take place over what is right or wrong. However, actual ethical choices and situations are almost always permeated with feelings and we ignore them to our peril. Three observations are in order concerning the role of feelings in ethics.

1. Feelings are those movements within us that draw us toward or repel us away from an action, a person, a thing, or an event. We are not raw intellect discussing blueprints to follow when we talk or think about morality. Some things attract or excite us; others

frighten or repel us. And there are myriad emotions in between: Our curiosity may be stimulated; a sudden disgust may fill us. These feelings are our primary connection with others and with our own actions. In fact, if you pay close attention to what you feel, you will often find that your reasoning is moving in an entirely different direction. You may be trying to justify what you know is wrong—but you want it. Feelings are integral to morals, or ethics.

2. Feelings are not just physical experiences or sensations in our bodies. They themselves come from somewhere; they have their own histories, their own stories. We like some things for many reasons, perhaps because we are familiar with them (our parents introduced us to them and we are comfortable with them), or because we get something special from them ("I like this"). Similarly, we may find that anger is a feeling we have learned ("just like Dad!"), even though we do not associate our angry response to problems as being remotely like our own father's. Notice, though, that anger doesn't just happen. It is learned. If feelings have histories, then it is important to know ourselves better by understanding something of where these feelings come from. But we must also remember that we are not the slaves of our feelings. We can understand them, follow them, or change them (though often with difficulty) in order to change our behavior. Feelings are part of our choices.

3. Psychology reveals more and more today about a gap between our conscious lives and our unconscious. Feelings are often buried in the unconscious layers of one's self. We may catch glimpses of these hidden realms—often frightening truths about ourselves, so we continue to hide them—but it takes a great deal of honesty (and sometimes some professional help) to acknowledge and deal with such feelings. At the deepest level, I believe we often discover our real sinfulness in this encounter, for we begin to lose the mask we offer to others as the "real me"—a mask that ironically only hides the real me. I find that when I pay close attention to my motives for various actions, there are often things going on under the surface that I would never acknowledge to others because I want them to know only good things about me.

"Create a pure heart for me" is the prayer of the psalmist. To me, the prayer arises not just for the forgiveness of sins (as if they were "things" to be removed); no, the plea is for the kind of wholeness that heals the split between the inner self and the person we try to make others, and even ourselves, see.

The next time you fall in love, ask yourself this strange question: Where is this feeling coming from? What is my real motivation? The feeling is not created by the beloved! It has its roots, its history in you. You may find an extraordinarily complicated mixture of feelings, motives, hopes, fears, honesty, and dishonesty. And, perhaps, you will begin to discover not how hard it is to fall in love (the feelings are real!), but how hard it is to have a pure love for this special person. Then you may learn humility in love and that, if I have read the mystics and the poets correctly, is the beginning of a responsible and honest love.

I conclude this chapter with a suggestion for a personal exercise. Spend tomorrow thinking about what you feel and where each feeling leads you (or keeps you from something). Try to forget about your thinking, your reasoning, your reasons for doing things. Concentrate on what you *feel*, where those feelings come from, and what they mean. Check how they influence your choices. Then share the results of your day with a friend. How well do you know yourself?

Questions for Reflection and Discussion

1. What does conscience mean to you? How does this fit in with what is presented in this chapter? Is there a difference between your conscience and your willfulness?

2. Think of a particular moral choice you have made. What role did principles or rules play? What role did feelings play? Were there any conflicts between the two realms or did they support each other? Explain.

3. In our society we have many heros, sports stars, musicians, political and business figures, saintly people. Name a person from each category and describe why they fit that category. What does each person teach you about choosing what is good?

4. Name one good habit that you have learned. Why is it good? Are there any weaknesses to it? What does it contribute to your character, to who you are?

5. Do strong feelings help or hinder your choices? Explain, using examples.

An Exercise: Who Is Choosing?

1. Think of two people who strike you as good people. What particular traits in their character are you attracted to? What makes these traits good? Are they moral traits, as opposed to other traits? What is the difference?

2. Name two aspects of character that you would like to develop as part of who you wish to be. (Note: Observe yourself as you share these traits. Are you embarrassed speaking about them to your peers? Is there a danger of ridicule, of being a goody two-shoes, we used to say, and does that change what you would say or how you choose to live—or not live—these traits?) Are there some traits that are safe to share and others that are not? Give examples. What does this tell you about the way we influence one another's behavior (and, perhaps, morality), and how that shapes who you are?

3. Think of a decision you had to make during this past week that forced you to think, perhaps sweat, a little. Can you describe the role of your conscience in making this decision? Again, think of a person or persons in a story who had to make a tough decision. What caused the struggle? What role did conscience play for this person? How do you know? Tell a story about someone you know, using the story to reveal what is special about this person (without drawing the moral yourself).

4. How do you feel when you do something wrong? Is this different than how you feel when you do something embarrassing? Where does conscience fit into this array of feelings?

For Further Reading

Callahan, Sidney. *In Good Conscience: Reason and Emotion in Moral Decision Making.* San Francisco: HarperCollins, 1991. (A good look at the various aspects of conscience, with a serious inclusion on the place of feelings in moral choices.)

Crossin, John W. *What Are They Saying About Virtue?* Mahwah, NJ: Paulist Press, 1985. (A good summary of the meaning, interpretations, and place of virtue in ethics.)

Hauerwas, Stanley. *Character and the Christian Life: A Study in Theological Ethics.* 3rd printing with new introduction (1985). San Antonio: Trinity University Press, 1975. (This technical work attempts to move moral theology back to a basis in character and community. The place of the moral law is not very clear, but the challenge to include more than law is profound.)

Keane, Philip S. *Christian Ethics & Imagination*. New York and Ramsey, NJ: Paulist Press, 1984. (This book is a serious attempt to go beyond our legal ways of thinking by incorporating an active imagination into our ethical reasoning. Very thought-provoking.)

Porter, Jean. *The Recovery of Virtue: The Relevance of Aquinas for Christian Ethics*. Louisville: Westminster/John Knox Press, 1990. (This is another study of Aquinas's ethical thinking. It concentrates on his appropriation of the classical theological and moral virtues as a foundation for the moral life. A good philosophical study of the place of virtue.)

Thomas, Laurence. *Living Morally: A Psychology of Moral Character*. Philadelphia: Temple University Press, 1989. (As it suggests, this is a psychological and philosophical look at ethics with a strong emphasis on the place of love and friendship in the formation of character.)

Chapter Four

Patterns of Moral Reasoning

The previous two chapters have introduced us to two kinds of moral theory: a theory of principles (or law) and a theory of virtue. While the theories often develop separately, they really need each other for a richer understanding of ethics. At this point we need to spend some time examining the moral reasoning that actually takes place when we have a problem and need to make a particular decision. Virtue and character often fall out of such discussions—but only because they are taken for granted. Can you imagine what it would be like to make a good decision with a friend who was a compulsive liar? Similarly, while rules or principles are often presented as the foundation for moral reasoning, actually applying them to a given situation in a manner other than legalism is the entire art of moral reflection.

Reasoning Proceeds in Certain Patterns

When carpenters build a house, they usually begin with a set of blueprints. Because a house is rather complicated and its components intricately related to one another, the carpenters are constantly checking to see if they are putting the pieces together properly. Occasionally, a sharp-eyed carpenter will notice that something does not make sense in the blueprint. Then, either the architect must be consulted or the carpenter must decide how to adapt the blueprint to fit the reality. A process of reasoning is called for that views the problem within the context of the entire house. For example, adjoining bedrooms may have had the closets mistakenly designed to share one space; a simple adjustment would put them side-by-side.

Applying ethical rules and principles is a bit like following a blueprint, but a whole lot different as well. If we have a set of clear principles to which we have committed ourselves, the process of living those principles every day is complicated by the many different situations in which we have to apply them. Thus, for example, I may believe fully in the maxim, "Be honest." In fact, for the most part, I may even follow that command in my relations with others. I do not tell bare-faced lies. However, I know myself well enough to know when I will "stretch the truth" in order to make myself appear better than I am. (Am I still being honest?) Even more, I also know where a lie could be quite profitable for me.

But what would you say to your best friend's mother in this case? Your friend has been caught vandalizing something in the school and has asked you not to tell anyone, especially his parents. You assume that he will tell them himself. A couple of days later his mother asks you if you know anything about the incident. If you want to be honest, but also true to your promise, what do you do?

It is sometimes very difficult to apply the principles we believe in most firmly. At times, it seems like obeying one principle will mean breaking another. At other times, one wonders if a particular principle is meant to fit all cases (Does "Do not murder" apply in time of war?). And occasionally it seems as if the details of a particular case make the application of a principle seem almost contradictory (as when an invading army demands from captured patriots "truthful" responses when interrogating them). Finally, there are situations where there is genuine confusion or uncertainty as to whether or not a particular principle applies in a particular case. (Should a doctor be honest with the patient's family members when the patient has explicitly forbidden the doctor to tell them that he has AIDS?)

Most moral principles do not provide automatic responses to every situation. Of course, the reason that they are principles is that they do give general guidance which does apply in almost all situations. Learning to reason morally is the art of making good decisions under this guidance. Human beings instinctively try to justify their actions, which means that they are trying to convince others (and themselves) that what they have chosen is good, or right. Even small children do this when they try to explain to their parents why they did something, like draw on the wall. It may also be appropriate to point out that we often try to justify bad actions or borderline actions through what is called rationalization, which puts an intriguing twist on being "rational."

As a subject of formal study, ethics has always sought to trace the patterns of moral reasoning in order to assist us to understand how moral principles apply in particular situations. Good moral reasoning examines every aspect of a case in order to ensure that there are no logical errors present and that the conclusion follows reasonably from the principles and the facts.

As important as it is to be logical and consistent, moral reasoning is unfortunately often reduced simply to logic and consistency. Accordingly, I would like to show how most of our day-to-day moral reasoning includes coherent justifications but only in the context of many different ways of learning and testing our ability to apply and live our principles. Based on the insights of the previous three chapters, I now offer six examples of moral reasoning. (Note: These are not six mutually exclusive ways, nor are they the only ways to reason morally. Often they complement one another while providing different perspectives on the same situation.)

Pattern 1: Using Moral Arguments—An Example

Over the past twenty years a moral principle has been established in medical ethics which now plays a significant role in decisions about the treatment given to patients near the end of their lives. The principle states, "When a patient is dying, then it may be appropriate under the correct circumstances to withhold or even withdraw medical treatment." Proper moral reasoning first demands that all the parts of this principle are correctly understood. However, in order to understand the parts, some of the historical context may be helpful.

Fifty years ago, the majority of North Americans died at home in their own beds. Today almost 70 percent die in a hospital. Fifty years ago treatments that are common today, like antibiotics for pneumonia or ventilators to aid a patient's breathing during a critical period, were unheard of or quite primitive. The proud progress of medicine as it pushed back the imminent hand of death for many people has, however, developed a shadow side. Many elderly and other critically ill people today can be kept alive long after a natural death might have taken place. By patching a heart, stopping pneumonia, repairing part of a bowel, doctors are able to keep death at bay. However, when a person is dying and the process is irreversible (that is, whatever is wrong with the person cannot simply be repaired, thus allowing the patient to return to a previous state of health), medical personnel have found that fixing one part of the body while the rest of the body continues to deteriorate may do nothing more than make the dying process more agonizing. The question then arises, "How much treatment should a dying person have?"

Morally speaking, one must first ask when treatment ought to be given. If the goal of health care is to save lives and overcome all ailments, then presumably treatment should be given if either of these goals can be accomplished. As medicine has become more technologized, however, doctors and nurses began to discover that many patients were simply being kept alive on machines, often in severely debilitated states that the patients themselves did not want. Still, if you can think like a doctor for a moment, what would it be like not to treat a dying patient, at least with a technique that *might* do some good? Or what would it be like actually to turn off the machine that is keeping a patient alive ("pulling the plug")? Are you abandoning the patient to death, or perhaps even killing the patient?

It was at this point that ethicists stepped in to analyze the circumstances that are peculiar to the dying. They asked if the goals of medicine (healing, restoring, and caring) change for the dying person and if a judgment about treatment would be different where the patient is in an irreversible process of dying. To make a long story short, ethicists argued that any treatment that was either ineffective, or did little more than prolong the dying process, or was too burdensome to the patient could morally be refused. Treatment under these circumstances is more like an intrusion than a benefit. A dying person who is not likely to get better must still have the kind of care which is appropriate for the dying. In hospitals this generally goes under the title of palliative or comfort care. Highly invasive treatments, like surgery or chemotherapy, may do nothing more than make the dying of the patient more painful and less spiritual. Instead of concentrating on how to live while dying, the patient may well end his or her days struggling with additional sickness, pain, and anguish from the treatment. Notice, however, that ethicists do not say that the patient is dying from "a lack of treatment," but that the dying process is allowed to complete itself without too much interference from technology and medicine.

Obviously, this principle makes for some very tricky decisions. One patient, for example, may refuse a treatment as too burdensome (as is often the case with chemotherapy), where another patient will try anything. A third patient may not want to prolong her dying, while a fourth sees every extra day as a day of living. Still, what is important here is to realize that *under some circumstances* it is perfectly moral, and therefore a legitimate option, to refuse treatment that only interferes with dying.

Furthermore, the ethicist argues that if it is moral to withhold treatment under the right circumstances, then where the same circumstances hold but the treatment has already been begun, it is still moral to withdraw the treatment. (One of the reasons for this moral equality is simply to allow doctors to begin a treatment which they do not know will be hopeless until they have more information about a patient's condition.)

Go back to the statement of the principle. Notice how every part of the principle counts. It is not a blind statement that the dying will have no treatment. The principle allows for situations to be recognized—usually on the basis of the patient's own decision—

wherein hi-tech, invasive, or even relatively simple life-prolonging measures may be refused. The phrase "under the correct circumstances" is a catch-all phrase which reminds us that this principle is not like the carpenter's blueprint. To be overly brief, the correct circumstances include the specification "when a patient is dying," since the refusal of treatment by an otherwise healthy person could imply that the patient wants to die and has found a convenient way to "allow" death to happen. For example, a person with pneumonia can easily be cured with the proper antibiotics; a young man who is despondent from a failed love affair suddenly comes down with pneumonia and decides that he will die by refusing treatment. That choice would not be moral because he is intending his own death, even if it is the pneumonia that kills him. He is not truly dying *unless* he refuses treatment.

An ethicist could sit down with this principle and go through typical cases encountered in a hospital and argue where it might apply. A person whose kidneys have failed so that she must now receive renal dialysis (a treatment which does the blood-purifying work of the kidneys) three times a week knows that if she stops dialysis she will die. But is she dying already? One could argue that she may live for many years on dialysis or until a kidney transplant can be performed. If so, then she is not at liberty (that is, morally justified) in refusing dialysis because then she would certainly die in a week or so. Suppose, however, that this woman were also suffering from bone cancer, a terminal illness. She would be dying and it would be her decision, if she so wished, to stop renal dialysis rather than die from the cancer.

These are difficult choices, for even an 80-year-old person may want to live much longer. That is why the principle is interpreted as a choice about *treatment* that is too "burdensome." While outsiders (like ethicists, doctors, nurses, and family members) can discuss what the treatment is like, only the patient can judge when it becomes too burdensome. Chemotherapy for cancer patients is a good example of treatment which, for some patients, is worse than the cancer. The patient must know the prognosis, that is, the possibilities or "odds" a treatment option offers in order to make the immensely personal decision about refusing treatment. (Note that to refuse invasive treatment does not mean that one refuses *all* treatment; palliative care provides pain relief and comfort care for the dying.)

We may conclude by noting how important the moral principle is. People have a perfectly moral option, when they are dying, to avoid any treatment that is ineffective, only prolongs their dying, or is too burdensome. They do not have to be "trapped" by hi-tech medicine. However, making the *correct moral decision* means more than simply applying the principle. All the factors surrounding each individual case must be taken into account before a particular decision can be made. The art of morality, and of living, is to make a good choice, one possibility of which is protected by the principle itself.

By way of contrast, we might ask ourselves whether or not a woman should be able to ask a doctor to kill her if she is dying anyway. The principle we are considering would not allow this because instead of allowing the dying process to complete itself, some person would have to intervene and actually kill the patient. Thus, the whole moral tone of the case would change. Now there would be a killer and a victim. Of course, some people may ask what the difference is between allowing someone to die (often in a slow, drawn-out process) and quickly ending the person's life. "Surely, a quick death is preferable to a slow one," they argue. Notice how this argument takes the principle on withholding or withdrawing treatment to the next step of actively ending a patient's life. But active killing is not covered by the principle. So, a whole new set of arguments would have to be presented as to why or why not killing a patient is a moral option. But that is a task for another book. One ethical quandary invariably leads to another.

In summary, moral reasoning tries to accomplish three things:

1. Moral reasoning seeks to make the moral principle as specific and clear as possible.

2. Moral reasoning explains how the principle fits and where it does not apply. The logic of the principle and a coherent application are extremely important here.

3. Moral reasoning weighs the arguments from both sides in order to ensure that the principle is applied in each particular case as reasonable or good.

Moral Reasoning: Questions and Exercises

1. Review the arguments that support the principle for withholding or withdrawing treatment that a patient finds too burdensome. Are there any other facts or questions that ought to be considered both in stating this principle and in applying it?

2. Assume that a good principle for sports is "Do to others as you would have them do to you." Could you formulate this principle to apply to one of the pickup sports you play, baseball or hockey or basketball, or to any gathering of young people? What are the problems often encountered in this sport or this gathering that a good rule might help overcome? What are the reasons for implementing the rule? What would be some counterarguments?

Pattern 2: Case Studies

Once moral principles have been established and made clear, particular cases may be presented to see whether and how the principle fits. In medicine, case studies often push a principle to the limit, but they force our ethical thinking to face the messiness of living.

Recently a teenage boy in Massachusetts was diagnosed with leukemia. He was put on chemotherapy and other treatments and told that he had an 80 percent chance of a complete cure with this treatment. After several doses of the chemotherapy, the boy begged that the treatment be stopped. When the doctor and his frightened parents refused, he fled to Texas where he promised to return home only if he was not forced to undergo any more chemotherapy. He returned home and died several months later. Was he morally justified in refusing the treatment?

This case differs from the usual cases where the principle of withholding or withdrawing treatment is normally applied. A teenager has his whole life ahead of him. He was offered an 80 percent success rate, a very good prognosis in regard to cancer. And the admittedly brutal side-effects of chemotherapy would disappear within months after the end of his treatment.

This is a tough case because of these circumstances. Whether the boy was justified in refusing treatment or not, perhaps only he could say. After all, the principle speaks of treatment which is "too burdensome." An outsider might accuse him of being weak or even cowardly in the face of the treatment.

But three other factors need to be considered. First, because he was a minor (that is, under the legal age for making his own health decisions), his family and his doctor must have faced the possibility of forcing the treatment on him against his wishes. If parents are going to be good parents, they occasionally have to inflict something on an unwilling child, such as vaccine shots for a child who hates needles, in lieu of serious disease. Should the teenager's parents have forced him, so to speak, to choose to live? And, second, one could ask whether he really understood the choices before him, death by cancer versus an 80 percent chance of being fully restored to life. How would a person know whether or not he really did understand? And, finally, was he dying? That is, can we say that the principle on withholding and withdrawing treatment was valid for him because the principle applies only to those who are dying? (We may note that *legally*, at least if he were not a minor, any person may refuse any treatment at any time. We are, however, asking the question about a morally acceptable refusal.)

Such case studies force us to face other principles about health care. The principle of informed consent demands that the teenager know exactly what his options are. The principle of parental responsibility requires that the parents exercise their best judgment concerning the care of their son. The moral responsibility of the physician demands that he or she help the young man rather than abandon him to death by cancer.

Furthermore, some of our definitions come under careful scrutiny. For example, when can we say a person is dying? Isn't someone with a serious cancer certainly dying? Or must we say that he would only be dying if he did not seek treatment? Case studies remind us that because of the variety of human situations to which the principles may be applied, moral principles often carry that additional phrase "under the correct circumstances."

Case Studies: Questions and Exercises

1. Return to the example of a game or gathering that you recently were part of. Were there any differences in opinion about how certain rules applied? Think of any arguments that might have taken place. What was the argument about: that the rule was broken, that somebody cheated, or that an unusual situation arose that nobody

was quite sure about interpreting?

2. See if you can outline a case study from some ordinary activity. Present the problem, along with the principle or rule that should solve the problem and, finally, the arguments for applying the principle or rule.

3. Here's an exercise that might prove interesting. Do a case study involving only females and one involving only males. Is there any obvious difference in reasoning or outcome?

(Notice how case studies force us to understand moral principles better, just as moral principles force us to think through individual cases carefully.)

Pattern 3: Stories

Case studies are like stories, but every once in a while a story is told not for moral analysis but in order to bring out the ambiguities that often accompany the gray areas of our moral lives. Ordinarily we would say that it is immoral to chop off one's own hand or foot. Several years ago a lumberjack headed off by himself into the forest to cut several large trees. One of the trees bounced when it fell and caught the woodsman by the foot, crushing both the foot and the ankle while pinning him to the ground. His cries for help were in vain. He reasoned that if he remained there very long he would die of shock and loss of blood. Since he still held his axe in his hand, he literally chopped off his crushed foot, stopped the bleeding, and dragged himself to where he could get some help.

Learning from Stories: Questions and Exercises

1. Was his action right or wrong? Can you think of a principle that he was following that would justify cutting off his foot? What would you do in that situation? What other factors are involved in the morality of this decision?

2. Stories are not always easy to analyze into tidy moral categories. Would it be right for one person to cut off his foot under these circumstances and wrong for another person in the same situation? Why or why not?

3. Can you think of a personal story that shows something of the ambiguity of living morally?

4. Pick one of the stories or parables told by Jesus or a rabbi (there

is a very strong Jewish tradition of storytelling). Why did Jesus or other rabbis use such stories to instruct people?

Pattern 4: Role of Motives or Intentions

Contrast two stories about two different people. A well-dressed man used to walk by a legless beggar every day. He would often make a grand show of putting $20 or more into the man's hat. The grateful beggar always had a blessing on his lips for this man.

Similarly, a tidily dressed but obviously not wealthy man walked by the beggar every day. He occasionally threw a coin into the hat; but mostly he walked by with his eyes cast down.

Which of these two men was performing the better deed? Obviously, this sounds like something Jesus would talk about because an observable action may have an entirely different meaning once the heart of the agent is known. For example, we might observe that the well-dressed man not only makes a big deal of his generosity, but it may turn out that his money has been gained by some illegal means such as drug trading. On the other hand, the poorer man may have a family to look after and several other elderly people who depend entirely upon his wages. He never has much more than a quarter left over. In other words, much as Jesus pointed to the poor widow's small offering of two coins and commented that "she has given much more than all the rest" (Luke 21:1–4), so are we invited to be aware of the motive, or intention, behind any action before we judge whether the action is good or bad.

The intention behind our actions is, however, one of the most difficult things for us to pin down. The wealthy man probably does not himself understand why he is so generous to the poor. Is it to calm his conscience, or to make a show to others about his goodness, or is it possibly even a genuine concern for the beggar? For most of us, doing something for the sake of others depends upon unconscious but very real motives. Kindness to a person can be a plea for acceptance; disdain for another may be nothing more than self-disdain projected outward. Paying attention to our motives, our intentions, in our actions is a powerful key to prevent our morality from becoming an external, legalized morality.

Perhaps that is why so few of us see God, for one of the Beatitudes says clearly, "Blessed are the pure of heart, for they shall see God." Where our hearts are shrouded in secrecy and duplicity, the person or image I present to others will be far from the person within.

Discovering Motives: Questions and Exercises

1. Have you ever accused someone, or yourself, with the words, "You didn't really mean that!" The person may have hurt you and said, "I'm sorry!" But you either do not believe the apology, or you are yourself unready to forgive and so you refuse to acknowledge any sincerity in the apology. Can you think of one situation where you noticed this split between what someone, or you, said compared with what that person, or you, felt?

2. On the other hand, does a good intention change an otherwise bad deed? Give an example.

3. Think of a good deed you did recently. What were your *real* motives? Do you know?

4. Think of a bad action you did recently. What were your *real* motives? Do you know? Is there a difference in awareness between your motives for good actions as opposed to those for bad ones?

Pattern 5: Good Example

Among many of the Native Americans of North America, one may observe a pattern of teaching that is amazing in its simplicity. A father among the Woodland Cree teaches his son to trap not by explaining all the intricacies of setting and baiting traps, but by doing the work and taking his son along to watch. Almost everything is done in silence with the boy learning by practicing what he has learned through setting his own traps. The boy learns not only the techniques of trapping but also begins to see how his father reverences the land and the animals that sustain his family. Instinctively, the boy will learn not to overtrap, which would endanger the livelihood of the family. And he will value the mysterious union of humans, land, and animals according to the patterns learned by generations of hunters and trappers who have gone before him.

Most moral teaching takes place through good example. In our society, teenagers and young adults may argue with their parents about what is right and wrong, but when young people see the goodness (or the badness) of those closest to them, a seed is planted.

There is always a level of trust operative among people we love and care about. That trust opens doors for imitation. What appeals to us in another we are more inclined to choose, to imitate. The kindness of my mother, the uplifting humor of my father, the loyalty of my best friend—these and countless other deeply personal relationships form and mold me, especially when I trust the other person's goodness.

Receiving and Giving Good Example: Questions and Exercises

1. Name one person, or one attribute of some person, that you would like to imitate. What prevents you from being like that person right now?

2. Have you ever tried consciously to imitate the walk or the talk or the look of a celebrity or some other special person? Why would you do that? Are you as conscious of imitating the goodness of another person? Why or why not?

3. Tell a story of a good example that you received from someone you respect and trust.

4. To learn from experience, ask if anyone in your class or group has experienced the actual dying of a close member of his or her family. Ask this person (or persons) to be quiet and listen to the rest of you discuss two questions:

a. What happens when a person is dying? What can be expected of the dying person? What can be expected of those gathered around the dying person (family, friends, medical people)? What can be learned from a dying person?

b. Does any of this apply to your image of your own death? Do you have any particular fears about dying? Since death is almost a taboo subject for most of us, watch and see if the talk about death is somewhat remote.

Now invite the person (persons) who attended a dying person, and perhaps the funeral, to tell the story of both the death and his (her) own response. Remember that this is only one account of a death. What does an actual story tell you about the difference between theory or abstract talk about death (which has its value) and the actual experience of a person's death?

Notice that the "ethics of dying" is not simply about what medical treatment to accept or refuse. More important is the caring and sharing that occurs during the dying process. That is where the "good decisions" are made. Ask those who experienced a person dying what good decisions were made.

Pattern 6: Trusting the Voice of Authority

When I was a youngster the voice of authority, usually communicated by my father, was more than enough to get us to do something. I admit that much of the authority hinged on fear, for punishment was never far behind failure to comply. Nevertheless, I also remember when, as an eight- or nine-year-old, I helped my father tear down an old house in order to salvage the lumber to build our garage. I recall how he would explain something to my brother and me, and we would go to work with enthusiasm and a sense of accomplishment. Dad would pat us on the back when we finished and assign the next task. It was my first experience of being treated like one of the men. The trust my father showed in us was repayed in the work we conscientiously performed at his direction.

Today there seems to be less respect for parents and elders in general. I honestly admit that some of the fear is gone, which is good; but the wisdom and guidance that women and men of experience can offer their children is often also lost. Nonetheless, throughout human history (and still in most cultures today), the voice of the elder is often the most important element in moral direction. Parents communicate their values to their children. Venerable public institutions do not have to be re-invented every five years in order to carry out the law or run the country. Of course, both parents and governing authorities need to be questioned and corrected now and again, because they are not perfect. But there is much wisdom to be found among those who have journeyed before us. Our own parents were teenagers not too long ago, even if it may sometimes seem as if they have forgotten that part of their lives.

Perhaps because children are too close to their parents, they often do not appreciate all that their parents know, the wisdom they have gained. It is striking to watch a young woman or young man stumble onto the first teacher whom she or he thinks has all the answers (or, at least, an awesome proportion of them). It is also striking how often children grow up when they bear their own children and find out that their parents knew a lot more than they were given credit for.

We cannot always prove every moral rule we ought to follow. We can, however, trust parents, teachers, spiritual leaders, wise friends, and other good role models to provide us with reasonably good guidelines as we grow up. The question we all need to face is this: When should I follow the voice of authority? When should I follow the inner voice of reason (or conscience)?

A military commander who has earned the trust of his troops has but to command in the heat of battle for his soldiers to obey him. A loving mother can confidently instruct her teenage daughter about what to expect at the prom. A trusted teacher may provide excellent guidance on a possible career choice.

The voice of authority is not always right simply by virtue of its position of authority. But what ought to be expected from those in authority raises a special responsibility for these figures, a responsibility that demands a trustworthy fulfillment of their roles. It is the trust, even more than the authority, that is the gateway to wise and moral decisions.

To return to our medical example, we need only note that doctors in our society belong to a profession with a very high moral standard. Most of us, when sick, place a strong trust in the skills of the doctor. We trust not only the technical skills but also the moral application of those skills. We would be horrified to learn, for instance, that the doctor performed an unnecessary operation because the insurance company paid a lucrative dollar. We trust the doctor to do what is best for us.

What advice, then, ought a doctor give regarding the withholding of treatment for a dying patient? One must be very careful here, because most people would accept the doctor's opinion as a medical opinion. However, what the doctor has to offer is an ethical opinion, that is, whether or not it is *good for this person under these circumstances* to forgo treatment. A good doctor would explain the options to the patient and then allow the patient to pursue his or her own choice, generally in conjunction with family members, and often on the basis of questions posed to the doctor.

In this example one may catch a glimpse of the potential for authority to be abused in guiding others. One can also see, presumably, how much we depend upon one another and how important the voice of authority may be for us to find our way.

Note that the voice of authority comes in many different tones. A man may listen to his doctor but ultimately trust only the advice of his wife; hers is an authority that has been built up over years of care and love.

Voices of Authority: Questions and Exercises

1. Who in your life speaks with authority? Why? What different kinds of authority can you recognize in your own acquaintances? Whom do you trust? Is there sometimes a split between authority and trust? Why?

2. Where does the voice of God's authority fit into this picture? How do we know we are "hearing" God's voice? What role does your church play in helping you hear and understand the voice of God?

3. What do you suppose is meant by the "authority of law"? How does this relate to the authority of parents or wise people or government figures? What is the difference between the "personal authority" of your parents or teachers and the "legal authority" of the laws of your country?

4. What is meant by the "authority of reason"? How does this relate to the authority of parents or the authority of law?

5. Think of an example or situation where the "voice of authority" (say, your parents), the "voice of the law," and the "voice of reason" all agree. Why do they agree? Can you think of an example where one or other of these "voices " would disagree? How do you account for this disagreement? Is there a way to harmonize the voices and overcome the disagreement? Explain.

Final Reflection: Riches of Life

Although we may be surprisingly adept in our moral reasoning when something (new) troubles us greatly, most of our moral reasoning flows less from our ability to use logic and see the consequences of our actions than from our instincts and built-in habits of many years. Our moral principles *and the conviction* with which we hold them stem from many sources, most of which are not always recognized or acknowledged, particularly in books on ethics. We learn most of our values from life, although we often learn to think, to systematize, to criticize, to evaluate, and to imagine new possibilities through the help of carefully written books and the instruction of learned women and men.

Formal books of ethics may help us discern patterns of thinking, logical consistencies, possible consequences of actions, and much more. Good novels, historical biographies, even tales of science fiction, however, may also stretch our minds to include the nuances of life that logic and consistency can never fully capture. The tales of Charles Dickens provide a richer feeling for life in England in the nineteenth century than all the laws passed by the British Parliament, although both give us some insight into the moral values and choices of the British people during that time.

Most of all, though, the lives of those nearest and dearest to us are like open books we often read all too unconsciously. We are not born into a vacuum. We take mannerisms, habits, styles of thinking and talking from those we know. Being attentive to these multiple influences upon us will help us recognize more clearly what we are choosing and why. But we shall never know *all* the influences upon us, much less upon any single choice we might make. Accordingly, we need now to spend some time looking at the influence of the social context on our choices, first, to recognize how much we are a product of a much larger world than our own personal choices, and then to understand how we can influence that larger world and not simply be slaves to the powerful forces that shape us.

For Further Reading

Ackerman, Terrence F., and Carson Strong. *A Casebook of Medical Ethics.* New York/Oxford: Oxford University Press, 1989. (Medical case studies are presented in considerable detail to bring out the difficult ethical decisions required. Some commentary is found at the end of each chapter.)

Ashley, Benedict M., and Kevin D. O'Rourke. *Ethics of Health Care: An Introductory Textbook.* 2nd ed. Washington, DC: Georgetown University Press, 1994. (This is a textbook on medical ethics from a Christian perspective. It combines numerous ways of approaching ethical issues, including discussions of principles, case studies, and reflections on the meaning of health care.)

Harak, G. Simon. *Virtuous Passions: The Formation of Christian Character.* New York and Mahwah, NJ: Paulist Press, 1993. (An interesting work, making use of Thomas Aquinas, on cultivating the "good" passions that drive us toward good actions and compose much of our good character.)

Shea, John. *The Challenge of Jesus.* Chicago: Thomas More, 1975, 1984. (Shea is a storyteller who lets the stories speak for themselves. He reminds us that the gospels are the story of Jesus and far richer than the efforts theologians often make to systematize this story.)

Shea, John. *An Experience Named Spirit.* Chicago: Thomas More, 1983.

Shea, John. *Stories of God.* Chicago: Thomas More, 1978.

Stivers, Robert L., et al. *Christian Ethics: A Case Method Approach.* Maryknoll, NY: Orbis Books, 1989. (A challenging set of reflections on major moral issues; theory and individual case studies are tied together.)

CHAPTER FIVE

WE ARE SOCIAL CREATURES

While individual decisions can be analyzed in many ways for their rightness or wrongness, we risk the danger of misunderstanding individual actions if we isolate them from the world in which they take place. The social world in which we live permeates every individual choice. To understand our choices we need to be aware of their context.

During the early part of this century there was a missionary who worked among the cannibals of Papua-New Guinea. When the First World War broke out, he was recalled to Europe to look after the soldiers as a chaplain. He explained to the cannibals that a major war had begun and he needed to return home. Pressed on the issue of the war, the missionary detailed the gruesome stories of trench warfare and mass slaughter. The chief surprised the missionary by asking how the dead soldiers were prepared for eating. The missionary explained that such behavior was not civilized; the men were simply buried. The chief was horrified and exclaimed, "What is the point of killing so many people if you do not eat them?"

This little story reminds us of the different worlds of human beings. We all live in a particular culture which forms and molds us in ways we are often not conscious of. To the cannibal chief, the eating of war victims was taken for granted. To the missionary, warfare with its unbelievable power to kill and destroy was taken for granted. Each had "grown accustomed" to something barbaric—and mystifying to the other—within their distinct cultures.

Dominance of One Culture

In North America, a dominant white, European culture has been taken for granted. History courses have focused on what happened in Europe and the United States. White leaders and military campaigns, not black slaves, were seen as the "story" of this part of the world.

Today there is a much greater consciousness of the different peoples of the world, their various customs, and their distinct cultures. This fact of life has created a number of difficult questions for ethics, the most critical of which is a basic question about where ethics (or what is good) comes from. Does it come simply from the cultural norms and roles that grow and develop within a particular culture? Or is there some ethic or standard that holds for all human beings in all times and places?

A further profound question arises: What effect does a particular culture have on an individual's personal decisions? If we look at nothing more than statistics, we will see that inner-city children have a much higher chance of being involved in crime than suburban youth and an even higher chance of being killed before adulthood. It is obvious to everyone that one's upbringing has considerable influence on the kinds of choices a young person makes. Parents often have the blame laid at their feet when a child goes wrong. What is much more subtle, however, is to recognize the influence a whole society or environment has on the individual.

Environment and the Individual

Think for a moment on the kinds of influence that an inner-city youth encounters daily. There may be less parental supervision, more pressure from gangs, poorer schools and fewer expectations from education, relatively easy money in the drug trade, over-whelming violence and killing both on television and, often, around the corner. Even parents who are the most conscientious in raising their children have to put up with a constant atmosphere of fear and danger.

Now ponder for a moment the life of the suburban youth. Usually, this youngster lives in safety, goes to a clean and efficient school, has opportunities to play in organized sports or follow other hobbies, and often has to deal with a type of boredom associated with middle-class living. Ironically, some of these kids begin to steal for thrills or to get cash for living above their means, and so on.

In other words, both environments can contribute to good and bad in individual persons. Neither environment causes in any direct way good or bad in people, otherwise everyone would turn out the same. But the statistics remind us of the particular pressures and their effects upon individuals within any particular culture.

Tribal peoples often have ways of acting in accord with self-understood rules, norms, taboos, expectations, customs, and reasons. For example, northern Eskimos would never refuse to feed a guest in their igloo, even if the family did not have enough food for themselves. Hospitality is more important than self-interest, even in the face of starvation. Compare that with North American middle-class culture, where we often have more than we need. Visitors cannot expect to stay for a meal, usually, unless some prior arrangement has been made. The hosts might have planned only for their own family, for example, and would not have prepared enough food for everyone. To the Eskimo, such behavior is frightfully impolite and bad.

Social Context for Personal Choices

Analyzing the social influence on all of us is an incredibly complicated undertaking. Consequently, this chapter seeks to do no more than make the reader aware of the social dimension of morality. To that end I will present the following five points.

1. Who Is Guilty?

Unless we take account of the social dimension of our existence and the social influence upon our own individual choices, we may be guilty of reducing morality to individual and personal choices and actions for which only individuals can be blamed or praised. The one who does the evil deed, for example, is guilty and must be punished.

But compare these two situations: A teenager, Danny, from a normal, suburban middle-class family, holds up a convenience store and in a panic shoots the clerk. An inner-city teenager, Eddie, from a minority group, also holds up a convenience store and in a panic shoots the clerk. The actions, as seen from the outside, are exactly the same and both teens deserve equal punishment. However, if we look at the two persons involved—without trying to excuse either one because of environment or family background—we may find that the inner-city teen comes from a home where there is no father while the mother works twelve hours a day to feed her four children. Eddie got in with a bad crowd, wanted the things and the approval that others had, and to prove himself held up the store. Things went wrong and the clerk was killed. The boy has no second chance. The deed is done and the result is doubly tragic. Would Eddie have done this if he had been raised elsewhere? What other influences would have kept him from getting into that situation? A million things could be listed. Nonetheless, he made the decision. He pulled the trigger. And by law he has to pay for the decisions within his control.

The teen from the suburb, on the other hand, is what is often called, again from the outside, a bad kid. Danny wants a car and lots of money to do as he pleases. He doesn't care who gets hurt, although he tries to avoid anything that will draw the police. When things go bad for him, he uses his parents' shock, a good lawyer, and a suddenly squeaky clean image to show that it was a bad situation in which he "found" himself. In our society, statistically, he has a much higher possibility of a softer sentence than the inner-city teen.

Why? First, because he comes from a "more acceptable" background. Also, he has support within the structures of society (parents, a good lawyer, knowledge of the system) to play the system.

And, third, he is generally an exception to what one usually sees in the suburbs. The inner-city youth, however, seems to be just one more story like so many others. There is simply less likelihood that the resources and the energy (except, perhaps, from his mother) will be there to see that he is treated like an individual person in a way similar to the way the suburban teen is treated.

All the factors that went into the bad choices of these two youths had an immense influence, less on the actual killing of a clerk than on all the choices they made to be where they were when they killed another person. So much of the inner-city youngster's surroundings made guns, robberies, gangs, ritual proving, and the lure of money acceptable to him. That there are simply more killings under such circumstances is not a matter of statistics but of social influence. The statistics merely follow. Eddie, of course, is much more than a statistic—he is now also a killer.

In contrast, what can we say about Danny? Did his surroundings influence his choices? Or did he go bad *despite* his environment? Here we must be careful not to separate individual choices and their context. There certainly must have been influences on him. Perhaps he saw enough television to make robberies appear an easy way to get money. Perhaps his busy parents did not have enough time for him so he made his life elsewhere. Perhaps he was just greedy and chose a bad path. Both the influences and the personal choices are part of Danny. He did not make his choices out of a vacuum.

Meaning of Evil

Evil in our world is very difficult to understand. In fact, precisely because evil is evil it is irrational, that is, not open to full understanding. Seeing some of Eddie's and Danny's background might help us to understand how they got themselves in a situation where they killed someone. But it doesn't explain why they did it. In fact, if both or either of them is truly remorseful, it would not be unusual for them to admit that they simply have no idea why they did the deeds. Even to them it does not make sense.

Still they are each guilty of doing something that was wrong. Their acts were wrong. In fact, we can even say that what they did was bad, particularly in the light of another human being's death.

But how do we judge Eddie or Danny? Are they bad people? Do we have any idea what is in their hearts, what their potential for good is? Or what we would have done if we had lived in their shoes?

2. Actions Are Not the Whole of the Person

Thus, I come to my second point. We cannot judge any other human person. We see appearances; only God knows the heart. Awareness of social conditioning does not mean that we excuse evil deeds. Individual persons still have to make decisions. And as a society we have to ensure that individual actions are liable for the consequences. The law, theoretically, does not make any distinction between Eddie and Danny. Both killed an innocent human being and, theoretically, both should be punished equally for their actions. (How the law punishes in our society, that is, what good the punishment does, ought to be a thought-provoking question for some serious soul-searching.) Each of them could have chosen a different way. Each of them could have chosen not to pull the trigger, regardless of what they felt, what pressures were on them, or how they ended up in their situations.

What went on in each of these boys, however, is a mixture of a world gone awry and their own participation in that world. I repeat, the bottom line when we are tempted to judge another human being is to ask ourselves what we would have done in those shoes and with that background. We may feel horrified at what Eddie and Danny did; such response is natural to human beings. But that still does not give us the right to judge either one as simply bad. Like all of us, they are a mixture of good and evil. And as no one can take credit for all the good within, so no one can be assumed to be the sole source of all the evil within.

3. Structures of Good and Evil in Society

Let us for a moment direct our attention away from Eddie and Danny and back to the worlds in which they live. In every culture and society there are patterns of living, whether we call those patterns customs, habits, attitudes, conventions, expectations, or any of a dozen other names. Things are simply done or expected to be done in certain ways and according to certain norms. These patterns are referred to as *the structures of society*. Any gathering of people involves implicit structures. The more complex the grouping of people, then generally the more complex the structures. Tribal peoples do not need to write down their customs; they simply live them and the customs fit almost every situation they are likely to encounter. Consider, on the other hand, the structures of modern nations. We have local customs (in families, neighborhoods, at work, etc.). We also have huge realms of law (federal, state or provincial, local), as well as policies and protocols for work, business, the entertainment industry, etc. These structures guide us in the ways of doing things.

Such structures, though, do not fall out of the sky. They are put in place by human reckoning. Democratic governments are the norm in the United States and Canada because our history has made these the continual choice and expectation of our people. Or think of the groceries purchased at the local store; you assume that the listed weights are what they say. We have a complex mechanism in place to ensure that sellers do not cheat customers who have to trust the scales. Or have you ever watched cargo being loaded and unloaded at a dock? Have you ever wondered what kind of regulations and customs govern this orderly movement of goods?

Society—indeed, any clustering of people—cannot operate without structures. We may not like a certain set of structures, so we change them. But we cannot exist without them.

The problem, however, is that structures are the context within which individual human beings make decisions. And structures do not embody only what is good. The trade that we see on the cargo docks of a port city may well be governed by international trading rules that favor the wealthy and discriminate against the poor. Does the stevedore, who loads the ship, then have some moral responsibility for the evil done in an unfair trade that continues to impoverish the poor? Or consider the person whose job is a very simple one, packaging the landmines used by, well, who knows? It is a job, like others have their jobs. And perhaps the military of one's own country needs these mines for the country's defense. But the reality is that landmines are often sold at considerable profit to both sides of a distant war. And the vast majority of these mines kill or maim innocent civilians. Is the mine packager guilty of killing, or contributing to the killing, of innocent civilians?

We live in a world that is an astonishing mixture of good and evil. As a result, not only must we be careful in assigning individual guilt to people who do something evil, but we must also be aware that all of us participate in multiple ways in the very structures of evil that distort our world. We may be great boosters of the environment, for example, but think nothing of tossing candy wrappers on the street or throwing out literally tons of garbage per year to be disposed of who-knows-where. We think of ourselves in North America as hardworking, honest people in a well-to-do society, but few of us have any idea how much of that wealth comes from the production of war materials or unfair international trade.

Furthermore, there are many people who would justify our structures and subsequent actions as perfectly right under the circumstances. If we are going to have a prosperous society, we have to produce lots of waste. It is better than poverty. If we are going to be safe, we need plenty of military weapons. And on and on.

Structures of evil do not just happen. They are chosen because there is enough "good" (read: profits) in them *for someone* to keep them in place. Some structures are more obviously sinful than others, such as slavery or apartheid, although many people defended these structures for many years.

It is important to realize that changing the world is more than a matter of getting individuals to make better choices for themselves. Often the potential for good choices is so narrowed by the time they come to the individual person, that only one in a million people would make a good choice in that difficult situation. To make a better world we must also be conscious of these structures that play such a role in the very range of choices that are allowed us. And we must constantly attend to what these structures are doing, where they come from, whom they favor and whom they prejudice, how they can be changed, and perhaps if certain ones even need to be done away with entirely.

4. Social Justice

The process just described is one of the main works of justice or, as it is sometimes spoken of in the context of societal norms, social justice. A world in which there is blatant injustice is a world waiting to explode. As Pope Paul VI said in his famous speech to the United Nations in 1965, "If you want peace, work for justice."

Justice, as such, is an enormously broad and complicated field. It encompasses huge realms of social life: law, trade, human rights, equal treatment and equal opportunities, allocation of resources on an increasingly crowded planet. And justice touches almost every action between persons (as when a child proclaims, "That's not fair!" twenty times in a single day).

Accordingly, I shall pursue three relatively simple examples concerning justice in our society in order to show the social dimension of some of these issues and our choices.

1. Consider a business that sells its goods on the open market and so depends upon the price the market sets. Suppose the company sells cocoa products. Having discovered that the price of cocoa fluctuates, sometimes wildly, thereby affecting a stable profit for the company, its leaders decide to control the production and marketing of cocoa beans. Gradually, the company buys up the wholesale businesses that purchase all the cocoa beans in the world. Now the company is in control of its own resources—but also the availability of cocoa beans for every other cocoa company in the world. Suddenly, one company has a monopoly and there is no free market in cocoa beans. Despite pretenses (cocoa beans still trade on the world market as if different groups were competing in the sale of their products), one company sets the price and controls what can happen in the cocoa trade.

A free market system depends upon competition and more or less equal access to buyers. Somehow both this one company *and* the nations who allow it to trade from a monopoly have failed to protect the consumer, according to the stated premises of a free market. The company will argue, perhaps, that it is only trying to protect itself from wild fluctuations in the price of cocoa. Justice would demand that the company find a different way to protect itself, since a monopoly changes all the rules of the trade game in a way that favors only one player.

2. Consider a hotly contested issue in our society today, "affirmative action." Where, for example, only white males have been hired for certain well-paying jobs, the assumption is that a form of discrimination against women and minorities has been operating, often unconsciously. In order to allow for more equal opportunities for all citizens, the government demands that vacant positions be

filled first by women or minorities until a more just balance of workers is attained. The argument is that women and minorities ought to get preferential treatment now because the past has disbalanced their position so radically.

Now a white male may offer a counter-argument. He may say that now he does not have an equal opportunity to try for the same job, that he is being discriminated against *now* because other white men than himself got the good jobs before him. (This raises another question of justice: if all the candidates are equally qualified for one job, how should the successful applicant be chosen?) This case shows us two things. First, we see how complicated justice issues can be. And, second, we recognize that past injustices that are now part of the structures of society are not easily overcome.

3. Suppose your parents both work in a nearby factory. Everyone knows that the factory pollutes the air around the neighborhood, but nobody complains too loudly because the factory owners have let it be known that if they have to spend money to clean up their process they will close the plant and move elsewhere. When your parents' jobs are on the line, what do you do? This issue is a good example of the kind of compromises that are often worked out in the real world. Some pollution may be acceptable for jobs. How much is a tough question to answer. What is clearly right, cleaning up the factory, also has a cost, not just money but possibly also jobs.

Social justice may often demand, for example, creative thinking rather than an either-or attempt to solve the problem. The workers, perhaps, could offer to forgo a portion of their paychecks if the company and the government will raise the additional funds to clean up the plant. Justice is not "somebody's" responsibility; it is everybody's responsibility. And it is an essential part of creating a moral world.

5. Social Sin

Finally, we need to talk about "social sin." While the notion of sin has fallen out of favor in our society, sin itself has certainly not disappeared. Unfortunately, the notion of sin is often applied exclusively to the individual deeds of individual persons. Thus, robbing a bank is a sin; prostitution is a sin; angrily berating a fellow worker is a sin.

Is it, however, a "sin" for a business to pay its workers minimum wages? So-called sweatshops where immigrant women spend long hours sewing clothing often for a pittance per piece have long been a part of North American business. The shops are generally legal (just barely!), although they pay poorly, have awful working conditions, and provide no benefits to the workers. Supporters of these businesses argue that "the women can look elsewhere for a job if they don't like it here."

It is no coincidence, though, that most of these workers are immigrants, often with no education and poor English skills. Unions are actively discouraged and troublemakers and whistle-blowers are fired. Critics of the system speak of exploitation and oppression; supporters argue that jobs are provided. Most people would never work in such places, however, unless (or even if!) they were absolutely desperate.

Is there a sinful exploitation taking place here? Indeed, who would be guilty of "committing the sin" if the employers were simply trying to run a profitable business?

Social sin is only analogous to personal sin—that is, there are some similarities but major differences. Social sin parallels the "structures of evil" within society. Social sin is ultimately the result of individual moral choices by many different people. But it is much more than the cumulative effect of all personal sin; it tends to feed on itself. It is often a result not of personal sin alone. Market forces and those who manipulate the market, business people who follow the law but not necessarily the moral law, and scared citizens who sense an injustice but are unwilling to risk, for example, their standard of living in order to effect change—these and many other factors influence the presence of social sin in society. And through social sin human beings are dehumanized.

Social sin, in short, is the failure of a society to protect and encourage just opportunities for people to live fully human lives. Social sin cannot be eradicated by blaming some individual for the wrong. It must be exposed and challenged on many levels: political, economic, psycho-social, military, and, of course, personal, because greed, selfishness, corruption, and the like begin in the individual human heart.

Social sin is often felt as an oppressive power in the lives of ordinary people. It restricts their choices and it often contributes to further evil choices by desperate people. It can manifest itself in the violence of the inner city or the protective isolation and comfort of the suburbs. It can permeate business, unions, government, and family. Like all sin, it can bring us to question even God's goodness in a world that sometimes appears mad. But we must also never forget that if it comes from human choices, it can also be challenged through human choices.

Final Reflection: Parts of One Another

The unique, individual human person, in the thinking of North American culture, is accorded a dignity and a status that is often summarized in the notion of human rights. Each person must be respected by all other persons in ways outlined by declarations of human rights. "Rights language" has become part of the way of thinking not just of lawyers but even of young children who are not shy to assert "their rights."

There is, however, an attitude in much of our North American society that accompanies this notion of human rights: the idea that each individual human being is an isolated, independent, self-sustaining individual making his or her way through life by virtue of laws or agreements (such as "human rights") which keep other people from interfering with one's basic freedom. The individual becomes a survivor in an often hostile world by being strong, resourceful, and dependent on no one.

This image, as powerful as it is in our society, is really a myth, that is, an attitude imposed on society, or on our perception of society, as a way of putting some order into it. Such a myth is not unlike the attitude of ordinary people that movie and television stars are somehow better human beings or a better example of what it is to be human than the rest of us.

This myth of individualism contributes a great deal to the isolation of individuals in our society. It implicitly denies the social nature of human beings, in that it suggests a personal independence that may then negotiate a common life or community life to suit one's own wishes.

The reality of our lives is, however, that we are, first of all, social beings, that we actually learn who we are by growing up in families, learning a common language (within which we talk and think about ourselves), and sharing a common story with other people. A most helpful way to imagine this reality is to think of our use of language. Watch as a child learns to speak. If the child uses the wrong word to describe something, calling a chair a "twee" for example, the parents gently correct the child until a chair is called a chair. Similarly, grammatical corrections are ongoing as where "I" is taught to be used properly despite the child's tendency to say "me" wherever speaking of herself. Gradually the child learns to communicate in ways that others understand.

While language gives us much of our identity through our ability to talk and think about ourselves in relation to others, it also enables us to identify ourselves as individuals within the social fabric of society. We are not simply one part of a herd or one piece of a machine. We are self-conscious persons in the midst of other persons. Our rootedness in language (and other social connections) reminds us that we are more than isolated individuals trying to construct a society. We are a society or a community of individuals for whom human rights are an important protection within society, and our responsibilities within society can be summarized by the notion of justice or, perhaps, the Golden Rule.

To think about language, to pay attention to how we use words and language, to recognize how language connects us and, indeed, influences and even directs much of our thought and activities is to avoid many of the consequences flowing from a myth of independent individualism. Language, of course, is an opportunity for asserting our own unique individual personality, as great authors do when they write particularly good books or articles. But the book of an Ernest Hemingway or a Margaret Atwood is only possible because the language they use is first shared by other people. We are social creatures as much, or even more, than we are simply individuals.

Questions for Reflection and Discussion

1. Sit down with someone who is does not share your culture or background. What differences can you pinpoint in your eating hab-

its? In your ways of showing respect for your parents? In your ways of raising questions? In the things you enjoy doing or not doing? What influences can you pinpoint in each of these patterns of your lives?

2. What is justice? What is justice in your classroom or for your group? What are some specific examples of how it works or does not work? Can you pinpoint some ideas on how to improve just relationships in your classroom?

3. What are some of the structures operative in your school, on your sport team, in your community? What are the pros and cons of these structures? Is there something that strikes you as unjust, something you would be angry enough to try and do something about? What could you do? What would be a creative solution?

4. In your town or area, are there people with whom you generally would not associate? Why? Separation and division are often a sign of social evil, but they have a history. How did this separation or isolation come about? Is it just? What kinds of things could you do about it? Remember, think of creative (and practical) ideas.

Exercise in Social Thinking

Bring a newspaper to school. Pick out four or five stories that raise ethical issues. What structures do you recognize in the various stories you see? What aspects of these structures would you call evil, if any? Is the evil in some sense "necessary" for the structures to also do some good? What suggestions could you make for changing the structures to lessen the evil impact, while retaining what might be good?

For Further Reading

Curran, Charles E. *American Catholic Social Ethics: Twentieth-Century Approaches.* New York/London: University of Notre Dame Press, 1982. (The often overlooked Catholic social thinkers and movements of the United States in the twentieth century are introduced in this book.)

Haughey, John C., ed. *The Faith That Does Justice: Examining the Christian Sources for Social Change.* Woodstock Studies, 2. New York and Ramsey, NJ: Paulist Press, 1977. (Though slightly dated, this collection of articles provides a very good grounding from

Scripture and the Christian tradition for social understanding and involvement for Christians.)

Mott, Stephen Charles. *Biblical Ethics and Social Change.* New York/Oxford: Oxford University Press, 1982. (This is an attempt to plumb the Scriptures for a coherent and challenging social ethic.)

O'Keefe, Mark. *What Are They Saying About Social Sin?* New York and Mahwah, NJ: Paulist Press, 1990. (A concise and excellent summary of what is meant by social sin and the challenges it poses for ethics.)

Vanderhaar, Gerard. *Why Good People Do Bad Things.* Mystic, CT: Twenty-Third Publications, 1994. (This readable volume is a fine effort to raise consciousness about contributing to evil structures in society, even unwittingly.)

Too numerous to mention, but well worth pursuing, are the many books written by various liberation theologians: feminist authors; African, Asian and South American writers; voices of the poor.

CHAPTER SIX

THE FAITH DIMENSION

While the morality of an act or an omission can be examined by any reasoning human being, there is always a question raised about the place of religious faith in both moral reasoning and in moral theory. Does it change or perhaps even veto human reasoning? Does it add something—direct revelation from God?—to our moral choices? The first five chapters of this volume have focused on the human acts of reasoning morally. By paying attention to what we do when we make choices, by citing some of the aspects involved in our moral reasoning, and by tracing several of the patterns our moral reasoning follows we have introduced ourselves to our own moral thought. Now, as we consider what is often the most important aspect of a human being's life, the faith dimension, we need to understand where this profound dimension of being human fits into moral decision making.

Several months ago in a debate on euthanasia I (a Catholic priest) asked a question of a pro-euthanasia doctor about how he could know for sure that it was the right time to kill somebody. His "answer" surprised me. He said that I was entitled to my personal opinion, my religious perspective, on euthanasia, but I should learn to respect the opinions of others who disagree with me on moral issues. My surprise was the result of his avoidance of my question. I had asked a moral and a factual question about the criteria whereby a doctor would know who to kill, and who not to kill, should euthanasia be legalized. He turned the issue into a religious one and thereby avoided answering a legitimate, and essential, question on the issue. I had not asked a religious question. Nor had I presented a religious perspective or a religious argument. I had not said, "God forbids this," or "Our faith holds every life sacred." I had asked a moral question as a fellow human being.

What is most troubling behind the doctor's response—a common response in many moral debates—is twofold. First, his implicit claim or accusation was that I was entitled to my Catholic opinion (like any faith opinion), but I ought not to "impose" that opinion on the rest of society (sound familiar?). Second, he implied that a faith conviction is a "private" opinion, due the respect of all private opinions, but not something that should be offered for public debate on the state policies we call the law.

Unfortunately, this tactic is rather common. First, religion is "privatized," that is, banished to the realm of sensations and feelings, which are intensely personal. And then religion is deemed unfit for the "real" debate that other citizens will engage in concerning the rules of society.

And so the question is raised, what role should faith or religion play in morality and in legislation about moral issues? The question does not permit an easy answer. Still, it is important to understand something about religious belief and the role it plays in our moral convictions and in our common law.

Personal Faith and Religion

To begin, we need to distinguish personal faith conviction and religion. True religion begins with the personal belief of convinced individuals. Christians, for example, believe in Jesus Christ, the Redeemer, and his story. They accept his Way for their understanding of God and as guidance for their behavior. Jews believe in their calling to be the people of God, faithful through their observance of the Law. (There are obviously variations in these and all religious groups about how this faith is to be lived.)

Personal belief, however, is not simply to be kept private, within oneself, so to speak. Faith is to be shared, expressed in various ways with like-minded believers. Certain symbols come to express the belief; certain statements—creeds—summarize the content of the belief; certain rituals and prayer forms draw the believers together into a living relationship with God and one another; and these believers generally identify themselves with a way of living their belief. There are, then, many religions in accord with different perceptions of God, different traditions about God, and different ways of living for God. We need not minimize the reality of different world religions, nor of different denominations within every major world religion.

Nonetheless, for the individual who truly believes in God and follows a certain way of religious belief, many of the most profound convictions about being human and living in certain ways come from this religious adherence and conviction. When Pope John Paul II, for example, preaches that every person deserves the respect owing to the dignity of the individual human being, this "belief" comes from an awareness of God's loving creation of, and care for, each one of us. The statement is not an abstract declaration of a principle of equality (though it includes that); it is a living and powerful conviction about human beings because of a living and profound conviction about a good and loving God. Where others who "believe" in the principle but would not give it the depth that John Paul's living faith assumes, there could be a serious difference in the way the principle is applied. A utilitarian philosopher, for example, might be willing to sacrifice one human life (for example, a dying infant) to save other human lives (through organ donation). That the dying infant would have to be killed in order to obtain the organs in good condition (after all, the infant will die shortly anyway) might be possible for the philosopher (though this is a hypothetical statement), but it would never be possible for the believer. Dignity, and the corresponding right to live is not something an individual forfeits because he or she is dying.

In other words, while a fundamental moral principle can be expressed by two people in exactly the same words, what it means and what it encompasses depend very much on the profound convictions of each. A believer does not have to immediately set aside inner convictions in order to talk with others who do not share those convictions.

Religious Belief and State Laws

There is, though, a problem. If the members of a society wish to set common standards for the society, what role should religious conviction play? It is understood by believers as well as by others that no single set of religious beliefs ought to be imposed upon a society, unless everybody in that society shares those beliefs. It has taken Europe and North America over 400 years to arrive at an atmosphere of mutual respect and toleration of other religions and denominations within pluralistic societies.

Yet, if the imposition of one set of beliefs is impossible, it does not thereby follow that all religious beliefs must be set aside in order to come to common standards, whether in constitutions or particular laws, for that society. Those who do not share any religious belief, for example, are still believers. Atheists cannot prove that God does not exist; they simply believe that God does not exist.

Unfortunately, however, our society is so influenced by an uncritical attitude toward science and technology, as if these alone teach us what is factually true, and it is fairly common for our leaders to assume that any religious opinion should not be part of the public debate.

The response to that attitude is simple. There are common standards we must set as a society *for all the members of society*, including the religious believers. Otherwise, the *only* voice that is *not* allowed to speak is the religious voice. Obviously, since there are often differences of opinion among different believers and different religions, the point is to ensure that a pluralistic society is truly pluralistic, that is, listens to *all* the voices of *all* the members of society and then seeks to do what is best for the society as a whole. To exclude religious voices because they are religious, or to imply that they express merely personal or subjective opinions, is to misunderstand the place of faith in the lives of those citizens who are religious believers.

Source of Moral Conviction

Christians believe, and have good arguments for this belief, that God's law and the moral law are essentially the same. We believe that God has revealed in the Ten Commandments, the guidance of Scripture, and the teaching and example of Jesus much of what is good for us, of how we ought to live our lives. We also believe that much of what God has revealed to us can also be discovered and understood by right thinking. Thus, there are two approaches to moral debates in our society that Christians must always be aware of. On the one hand, our most basic convictions may well come from God's revelation. A Christian, for example, may be generous with the poor not because the abstract laws of justice demand this (although one could argue morally that they do), but because of the teaching of Jesus, which expresses an abstract law of justice in such terms as "we are all children of one Father in heaven." On the other hand, in a society where not everyone believes in Jesus, much less in a single God as father/mother of us all, the Christian must be prepared to argue the Christian case for the correctness of this view of justice.

Outsiders may accuse Christians of a form of schizophrenia, believing one thing and arguing on another level. However, the belief itself provides a unity. If we are so utterly convinced of the equal dignity of each human being because we know God as Creator and Father, then our conviction extends to the need for society to protect all human beings in accord with this principle. Because of the deep conviction of what we have learned from God about all human beings, Christians must oppose philosophical arguments that tend to weaken this protection, but by using arguments that philosophers may understand.

Christians, though, must never forget where their basic convictions come from. If they do, then they will have no tools to argue their case other than the arguments and the worldviews of the philosophers and others. And there is no telling where such theory will take the human mind that is not anchored in a living, personal relationship with God.

What role should our religious faith play in our moral convictions and behaviors? Neither faith nor a particular religious affiliation provides us with a list of moral laws and behaviors that we are to follow blindly. Faith gives us a perspective that encompasses our

world, our universe, our origins, and our future. Faith invests human living with a rich and varied meaning or, to say this more accurately, faith divines a meaning in the midst of human life. To take
a simple example, if faith provides a person with the conviction that
there is an afterlife (and a judgment for one's actions), then there are
consequences to one's moral choices that go beyond the justice of
this world, or the lack of it. One can serve God in honesty and truth
(or in fear of final judgment—both attitudes may be at play in a relationship with God), regardless of consequences, rewards, or self-
centered wants. Of course, a complete atheist could claim to follow
the same noble principles (which do not have to be expressed re-
ligiously) for his or her own inner convictions about being human.
(What those convictions might be, how they are justified, and
whether they can be lived without the assistance of grace known by
the believer is another question.)

The point here is not to say, "Well, what difference does God
make?" To the true believer, God makes all the difference in the
world because the standards for my behavior, for my moral choices
are set by God (a loving God who sets those standards for our benefit). I can trust them even when I am tempted to rationalize my decisions that go against God's instructions.

Christian Faith and the Language of Law

Law-language is one form of speech about moral living; instructions in right and wrong can be, and often are, summarized in
law statements. These may be very general, covering all situations
of human living, as in the two great commandments of love. Or
they may be more specific, but general enough to cover all appropriate situations, as in "Never murder another human being."
Or they may be formulated as rules or laws that hold in most cases,
or express some human wisdom about certain kinds of situations,
or are guidelines for virtuous behavior.

What is important to realize, however, is that law-language is not
the only, nor often, the principle way in which we learn to do and
be good. The teaching of Jesus is first and foremost conveyed to us
in the story of Jesus, captured by four gospels and explored directly
or indirectly in other books of the Scriptures. This story itself con-
tains stories and parables, wisdom sayings and instructions, par-

adoxes and laws, histories of persons and communities, plus other forms of human writing. In the richly complex manner of all human communication, the Scriptures and the story of Jesus seek to tell all who will listen how and why God wants to talk to a chosen people. The conviction that comes from this story, the personal relationship with Jesus which is called faith, the religious expressions of this faith by communities of believers, and, of course, the attempts to summarize instruction for our behavior according to the Law in all its richness are all resources for our moral convictions and choices.

Simply put, to do something out of love for God is quite different than doing something because the law says so. The actions may look the same; indeed, the results may appear to be the same. But the implications of the two are miles apart—which is not to say that we human beings cannot do things for both motives, as when we follow a law that we are not too sure about but that we believe is a revelation from God.

Role of Reason

The Christian, moreover, realizes that God has also given us an immensely ambiguous tool to assist us in living our convictions, namely, the gift of reason. Convictions may come from many places, despite claims that we are doing something out of faith. Reason is, then, a tool to examine what we believe and why, to reflect upon the purity of our hearts and our motives, to assess critically the logic and coherence of our positions. Furthermore, reason is a companion of the heart, not an enemy or an overseer. When properly understood and not arbitrarily restricted to scientific thinking or to "the facts," reason accompanies every dimension of human life, every aspect of human freedom, and therefore every bit of the moral life.

Reason may be summarized by habitual ways of doing things. Or it may tackle never-before-seen problems to understand what solutions may be possible. And certainly it has a special task in acknowledging and understanding, as far as possible, what Blaise Pascal called "the reasons of the heart." Reason is neither the opposite of faith nor the judge of faith convictions. It is the companion of the free and responsible human being, whether a believer or not. And for the Christian, the relationship of the two is summarized in the phrase "reason informed by faith."

Reason and Faith of the Community

Ultimately, the believer belongs to a community. And while academics argue about particular beliefs or laws and their justification, communities tend to live in certain ways that embody these beliefs and laws. In fact, much of what we learn in our communities is lived long before actual statements about these beliefs or laws are formulated. It is usually only when a particular doctrine or moral law is contested or challenged that summary statements are formulated and presented as approved. For example, in the early church the doctrine of the Trinity developed over a 300-year period in which first the divinity of Jesus was questioned and then that of the Holy Spirit. Formulas, credal statements, and theological writings gradually clarified what each phrase meant in claims about the Trinity until there was a general acceptance throughout the church. While the theologians and bishops argued, Christians generally practiced their faith in ways that implied the tri-unity of God. Community life is often a reliable expression of faith or morals where reasoning has not been able to draw clear conclusions.

Community provides much of the social context for the individual human being. The Christian community, as with any community, is like a womb where children grow, learn, and absorb the way of life that surrounds them. Ironically, some parents in the 1960s thought that they could "free" their children from imposed values, particularly religious ones, by allowing them to grow up without any faith community context. The theory was that the children would then be "free" to choose their faith when they were old enough. The reality was that the children still grew up in a context, but one in which God and what we know about God did not play a role. They absorbed the way of life in which they had grown. They were "free" to choose a faith, but they had no experience of it with which to choose. Community is a part of the social context that a person, or parents, can choose freely. And to choose not to educate one's children to know God is to assume that it is not important to do so. The million flavors of life that one absorbs in a community are simply replaced by a different social context of flavors. That is not having greater freedom. And that is nothing more than a different faith!

Authority in the Community

Within community there is also the reality of authority structures. Every community needs some form of interrelationship that respects different talents and responsibilities within the group. Since I am most familiar with the Catholic church, I will briefly point out some of the aspects and roles of authority within this community.

The most obvious figure of authority within the Catholic church is the pope. But authority within the church lies first and foremost with God. Popes, bishops, priests, teachers, and parents must all learn that their authority in a very profound sense comes from God. As no parents are absolute and able to dispose of their children as they wish, so no authority within the church has an arbitrary authority. Each level of authority must respond to the reality of Christian faith and Christian community. For example, the papal authority cannot contradict Scripture, for the Bible as the Word of God has a prior authority to that of the pope. Papal authority must serve God's Word.

Authority may best be understood as the wisdom of leadership, direction, and interpretation in an often confusing world. Authority provides leadership where competing voices would divide a community. If the community does not acknowledge a leader, someone will generally fill the void and take over. Authority gives direction where unity is needed along the way. Its special role is less to rule than it is to recall the community to what is authentic in its tradition. It guides by being wise about what is important and needed for present-day living in the community. And it has the responsibility of interpreting how God's revelation fits each new dimension of human history.

Think of some of the things that the world has forced us to make moral judgments about, things that are not, nor could have been, mentioned in the Scriptures: nuclear weapons, DNA testing, the use of computers, and so on. That the Scriptures do not speak specifically about these items does not mean that the wisdom of God's Word does not have something to say about how humanity ought to use such gifts. While everyone in a community has a responsibility to think about the wise and just use of any material creation, it may be the task of the community's authority to provide direction and guidance based on a correct interpretation of Scripture for the world.

Religious belief often provides its adherents with the ultimate meanings of life, death, human community, sin, and redemption. It does not have all the answers to all the questions posed by life. The sciences have much to offer, as do literature and the arts, folk wisdom and various cultures, skilled craftspeople and parents. Religion claims our special allegiance because of the profundity of its meaning, but it must be a partner in the pursuit of knowledge, including moral knowledge. Medical ethics is a good example where the artful techniques, for example, of surgeons must be combined with the care of nurses and other health care professionals, plus the ethical and often religious context of concern for the sick, in order to ensure that good is being done. These skills evolve slowly and in a mutual dialogue that seeks to ensure that the goal of good medicine, proper care of the patient, is always front and center.

Concluding Note
Religions and the State: Part of Each Other

Faith and religion are realities in the lives of people, important and often decisive. What is good for the citizens of a country who differ immensely in their religious beliefs is part of the political and moral process of legislating what is best for the citizens under these circumstances. To this end, religious values and moral positions ought not to be ignored, but acknowledged as part of the values of the citizens. Religious people themselves must learn to respect the lives and beliefs of others.

Sometimes believers must adhere to their most cherished moral positions only within their own community boundaries because the larger society does not acknowledge these moral values. The Mennonites, for example, and other traditional peace churches refuse to participate in war. That sounds very noble until a nation goes to war and then these people are often seen as not contributing their part to overcoming the enemy. How a nation deals with these people is, however, instructive in itself. In the past they have been thrown in jail, ostracized, and punished. Sometimes they have been allowed to become medics or volunteers responsible for anything that does not involve killing. Occasionally they have been acknowledged as prophetic in a world that increasingly turns to violence to try and solve problems.

How religion and state government relate to each other is a fascinating chapter of every country's history. That religious beliefs often challenge governments to be more moral, more honest, more just (and, occasionally, governments help to reform religious groups!) is simply one aspect of the role of religious belief within the morality of a society. That religious belief is often the cornerstone of individual decisions and actions should not be surprising. To live one's life out of a profound conviction of a loving and personal God provides motivations, strength, and endurance where merely human wisdom often fails.

Religion does not necessarily make better men and women out of any of us (we have to take the religious connection with God seriously for that to happen), but it is foundational for what is important in living our lives. For true believers, a relationship with God and a faith community provide the principal foundation for moral choices and deeds. This religious belief needs to be respected for its important role, rather than seen as an "add-on" to what it is to be human.

As I said earlier, those who claim to be atheists or non-believers merely believe in something else. Their opinions must be respected because of the dignity of each human being and the uniqueness of individual conscience. But, on the other hand, they should not be considered the model of what it is to be human such that the religious believer appears to be sneaking in something extra, something only subjective and personal. Belief in God and life within religious communities has much to offer not just believers, but any society that strives to be ethical in its actions and treatment of its citizens.

Questions for Reflection and Discussion

1. What does your own personal faith mean to you? Is there a difference between your personal faith and your religion? What are the connections?

2. How should your religious belief influence society? Do you think, for example, that:

a. There should be Catholic schools? Why or why not?

b. Religious views on pornography should influence the state to restrict such materials? Why or why not?

c. People should be allowed to run for government offices while acknowledging the importance of their religious faith? Why or why not?

3. What does your discussion of these issues tell you about how you view the relationship of religion and the state government? What role should your personal faith play if you hold an elected office in your government?

4. What does religion(s) do for government? What does government do for religion(s)?

5. Can you think of a moral issue that you hold very strongly *because* of your religious belief? Now, what kind of arguments could you raise to defend your position to someone who does not share your faith?

Exercises on Religion and Ethics in Society

1. Catholics and many other religious persons tend to be very strongly against abortion. They argue that life is a gift from God and no human being has the right, much less the moral justification, to end arbitrarily another human being's life. Society has chosen to legalize abortions for a number of reasons. What ought a Catholic to do when he or she, as a nurse for example, is called upon to assist in an abortion? What ought the state do to accommodate religious beliefs such as these?

Should Catholic hospitals allow abortions in their operating rooms for those who believe in at least the legality of abortion? Why or why not? What is at stake?

2. Jehovah's Witnesses believe that blood transfusions are immoral. If a member of this religious group has been in a car accident and needs a blood transfusion in order to survive, what should a doctor do who knows that this person would not accept a blood transfusion under any circumstances? What protection should the state offer the Jehovah's Witness? What protection for the doctor? Again, what is at stake?

Suppose the parents of a six-year-old boy refuse a blood transfusion for him, despite a life-threatening condition, because of their religious belief. Ought the doctor or the state to ignore the parents?

Who should make decisions for the health of a child? Do religious beliefs make any difference in terms of the care parents provide for a child?

For Further Reading

Catechism of the Catholic Church. Part Three: "Life in Christ." Washington, DC: U.S. Catholic Conference, 1994. (This section of the official Catholic catechism summarizes Catholic ethics from its foundations to many of its specific teachings.)

Curran, Charles E. *The Church and Morality: An Ecumenical and Catholic Approach.* Minneapolis: Fortress Press, 1993. (This modest volume raises a number of issues about Christian moral thinking in light of the different denominations and traditions of ethical wisdom in the Christian faith. Some good thoughts on the relation between faith and society.)

Furnish, Victor Paul. *The Moral Teaching of Paul: Selected Issues.* 2nd ed. Nashville: Abingdon Press, 1985. (A fascinating look at Paul's moral teaching in the context of his own times. A must for understanding the Scriptures.)

Gula, Richard M. *Reason Informed by Faith: Foundations of a Catholic Morality.* New York and Mahwah, NJ: Paulist Press, 1989. (This is a comprehensive introduction to traditional Catholic moral thinking. It provides a particularly good introduction to many of the fundamental aspects of moral theology from a Catholic perspective, which includes, necessarily, the natural law.)

Harakas, Stanley S. *Contemporary Moral Issues: Facing the Orthodox Christian.* Rev. ed. Minneapolis: Light and Life Publishing, 1982. (This book gives a very different perspective, an Orthodox Christian one, on approaching moral issues. It is quite illuminating to read alongside, for example, the Catholic tradition.)

Kelly, Kevin T. *New Directions in Moral Theology: The Challenge of Being Human.* New York/London: Geoffrey Chapman, 1992. (This is a less traditional attempt to outline Catholic moral theology in dialogue with many of the strands of ethical thinking current in the modern world. Thought-provoking.)

Spohn, William C. *What Are They Saying About Scripture and Ethics?* New York and Ramsey, NJ: Paulist Press, 1983. (One of the most insightful looks at ethics and its Scriptural sources. While the law dimension of the Scriptures is not overlooked, the other challenges for the Christian moral life are very well captured.)

CONCLUSION

Ethics, or moral reflection, is both more complicated than life and less. In order to reflect ethically, we often have to analyze the parts of an action, the meaning of human acts, the role and meaning of freedom, and so on. Compared to actually doing ethical deeds, the reflection can produce a royal headache. Nonetheless, in a sense one of the problems with ethics as a "thinking about" what we decide and do is that it must precisely simplify (or look at identifiable parts of) the ethical action in order to understand and analyze it. Accordingly, it may be easier for the ethicist to draw moral conclusions than for the person on the spot. The danger, then, of course, is that the ethicist thinks that the reflective answer is accurate before the reality of the situation is entered into with all its complexity and unique circumstances. Ethical reflection is meant, first and foremost, to supplement the ability of each of us to make good, or better, decisions. It is not meant to supplant or displace the reality of each person making his or her decisions ethically in the lived reality of daily life.

If we remember that ethical action itself invariably leads us, or even forces us, to reflect on what we are doing and why, then we will understand something of the symbiotic relationship between ethical activity and ethical thinking. The activity leads to the thinking, but the thinking takes us right back to the actual situation to make sure that it is understood as thoroughly as possible, before specific conclusions are reached.

Ethical reflection is not something to be feared, despite its perceived complexities. Even if there are complicated issues and troubling situations, human beings cannot avoid moral choices and actions. The point of this book is primarily to remind the readers of the naturalness of daily decision making and to communicate some of the complexity of our world and the decisions we face. We do need to think, and we need to think together, which means that much of ethical reflection is a dialogue, a discussion, through which as many as possible of the pertinent perspectives and facts on any issue will be raised.

Thus, we may conclude with the following reminders. Reason itself is a gift from God to be used to assist humanity in understanding and choosing what is right and good. Women and men of experience and wisdom ought to be fonts of moral knowledge and encouragement for all of us. Dialogue and discussion, learning from and sharing with others, is integral to finding and living good moral decisions. And, in the final analysis, women and men of integrity and authenticity, passionately prepared to pursue the truth and live it in humble awareness of human limitation, will be both the great teachers and the living examples of the best that humankind has to offer. In such personal and communal ways to "live the truth in love" does God's wondrous gift of freedom, given to all human beings, return glory to God.